The Rev. Prof. Beazley is an emeritus professor of Obstetrics and Gynaecology at the University of Liverpool. Prior to retirement as Dean of the Medical faculty, he trained for the Anglican Ministry at St Deiniol's Library, Hawarden, and has served as a non-stipendiary minister in the Diocese of Chester, Carlisle, and now Oxford.

His ministry has included the regular provision of study days, teaching seminars, and quiet days for those interested in understanding more about their Christian beliefs. His personal interest in *The Questions put by Jesus* stretches back over sixty years and has evolved steadily over that time.

Dedicated to the memory of my beloved wife, Barbara.

John Milner Beazley

THE QUESTIONS PUT BY JESUS

AUSTIN MACAULEY PUBLISHERS™

LONDON • CAMBRIDGE • NEW YORK • SHARJAH

A CIP catalogue record for this title is available from the British Library.

ISBN 9781398445918 (Paperback)
ISBN 9781398445925 (Hardback)
ISBN 9781398445932 (ePub e-book)

www.austinmacauley.com

First Published 2022
Austin Macauley Publishers Ltd®
1 Canada Square
Canary Wharf
London
E14 5AA

Table of Contents

Author's Preface

It sometimes occurs to me that, whereas most of us usually can be trained to perform straightforward practical procedures, it is only when we encounter questions that we really are led towards learning and understanding. It has been a real pleasure, therefore, to focus on the questions of Jesus and to explore what we can learn from them. The book has been written in the hope that it will be of interest to all who seek to understand Jesus as a person and his manner of teaching and ministry.

For the layout, I am indebted to the 1980s series *The Jesus Library* that established an excellent format for the teachings and sayings of Jesus. An internet search of recent literature suggested that a book on The Questions of Jesus in a similar style might be useful.

All the references are from the New Oxford Annotated Bible (New Revised Standard Version). The select bibliography seeks to acknowledge my debt to the excellent commentaries and other sources from which I have received great help in studying the biblical narratives. In addition, there are others whose teaching I have collected over many years in my personal notes and files. Their contribution has been invaluable, and I sincerely regret that because I failed to record their names at the time, I am unable now to acknowledge them personally.

I also should like to thank four local friends, Peter, John, Douglas, and Jim who encouraged this venture. We regularly engaged informally over coffee, and I am indebted to them for their stimulating discussions and the gentle manner in which they sustained my enthusiasm for the subject. If there is any originality in the substance of this book, the credit for its development belongs largely to them.

In closing, I should particularly like to express my heartfelt thanks to my daughter Ruth. Time and again she guided me safely through the mysteries of a computer which seemed to have a mind of its own! Without her endless patience, I should have fallen at the first fence.

John Beazley.

An Introduction to the Questions put by Jesus

It was about forty years ago when my attention was first drawn to "The Red-Letter New Testament, showing Our Lord's Words in Red." The idea was first conceived in 1899 by Louis Klopsch then editor of 'the Christian Herald'. He published the first edition of the New Testament later the same year, encouraged by his friend the Reverend Thomas DeWitt Talmage. I was fascinated by the discovery.

Here, suddenly, I could see a clear distinction between the words ascribed to Jesus by the Gospel writers and the general narrative of their text. Moving from one red passage to the next I was quickly impressed by the number of questions Jesus asked and interest arose which has never diminished.

As I gently pursued this interest, it increasingly became clear that despite the many excellent commentaries available to help with biblical texts, little attention had been focussed on the subject of Jesus' questions. It was evident, however, that asking questions was a significant feature of Jesus' ministry. Equally evident was that these questions were presented in numerous different forms and spanned a wide range of subjects.

They arose in debates and disputes with his opponents. They were prompted by discussion with his disciples or by statements from the crowds who followed him. Also, Jesus himself raised questions, usually when he was teaching in the Temple or the synagogues, or in his Sermon on the Mount, or during his great discourse with the disciples.

At first, it was interesting to reflect on how the echo of these questions resonated across the ages, how the thrust of them still probed our faith. To whom did Jesus' questions still matter? What did they still teach us about ourselves? Was their challenge still relevant to our time? Could we still identify with our Lord's situation in life? It was so easy to drop into the 'sermonizing mode'! But that, I soon realised, was far better left to more competent preachers. Instead, as my studies progressed, (I like to think it was progress), it became increasingly apparent that Jesus' questions offered an opportunity to explore far more than just sermons. They reflected the culture of his day, "Are not five sparrows sold for two pennies?" (Lk. 12:6).

They threw light onto Jesus' nature, both human and divine. They reflected his hopes, anxieties and disappointments. They disclosed interesting assumptions common to his times. Here was a belief in two different domains, one ruled by Satan the other by God (Mk. 3:22–26).

Possession by evil spirits was the cause of certain illnesses (Mt. 12:22–30 and parallels). Original sin was inherited from Adam (Lk. 11:11–13). Almost 'mechanically' sinful behaviour resulted in divine punishment (Lk. 13:1–5). And then there were the subjects of which Jesus never spoke, the religions that had not yet arisen and current global issues beyond the confines of his time. We can only surmise what questions he might have directed towards such matters.

Table 1. The order in which 189 Questions were examined.

	Questions Examined.	Parallel Questions (Not Re-examined.)			Total
1. Mark.	64	*	*	*	64
		|	|	|	
2. Luke.	60	(30) |	|	*	90
			|	|	|	
3. Matthew.	17		(48) |	(28)	93
4. John.	47	(4)			51
5. Acts.	1				1
Total	189				299

So, gradually, the purpose of this book took shape. It was to gather the questions Jesus asked; to focus on the types of questions he used, how he used them, and how they revealed something of himself, his teaching, his ministry, and of his relationship to others. Hopefully, this would help to shed light on his timeless question, "Who do people say that I am? Who do you say that I am?" (Mk. 8:27–29). Hopefully, too, some questions still would ruffle the feathers of our spiritual complacency.

How Many Questions?

It is not possible to be precise about the number of questions attributed to Jesus in the New Testament. Simply counting question marks is not the answer! Often the question is rhetorical, (not really deserving of a question mark!) In some texts, the same question is simply repeated, (Jn. 18:4–8). In others, depending upon the translation, the text (e.g., Lk. 11:5–8) is presented either as a question (RSV) or as a statement (NRSV).

Approaching the Gospels and the Acts in the order in which they usually appear it is reasonable to suggest that there are 93 questions in Matthew, 64 in Mark, 90 in Luke, 51 in John, and 1 in Acts: a total of 299 questions. Many of these questions, however, are similar and are repeated in parallel narratives in the different Gospels. It is not particularly useful, therefore, to examine them more than once. Accordingly, a slightly different approach to the subject has been taken in the present study.

Taking the Gospels in what probably is their chronological order, Mark, Luke, Matthew, and John, it is evident that of the 64 questions in Mark, 30 appear as parallels in Luke, 48 as parallels in Matthew, and 4 as parallels in John. The questions in the parallels, therefore, have not been re-examined unless there was good reason to do so. A similar examination was then made of each of the Gospels in turn, also the Acts. Using this approach, 189 unrepeated questions were revealed, and these have formed the basis of the present study (Table 1).

Interestingly, this chronological approach to the Gospels also reveals something of the attitude of each of the evangelists to the Jesus event and the questions he asked. Mark's Gospel, for example, has little hesitation in attributing ordinary humanity to Jesus in such questions as, "What is your name?" (5:9), "Who touched my clothes?" (5:30), "How many loaves have you?" (6:38), "Can you see anything?" (8:23), "What were you arguing about with them?" (9:16), "How long has this been happening to him?" (9:21), "What were you arguing about on the way?" (9:33), and "What did Moses command you?" (10:3). Luke's Gospel is not too dissimilar although the author tends to soften Mark's approach wherever he can.

By contrast, Matthew omits these and other questions in Mark (Mk. 8:12, 9:12, 10:6), and John often presents Jesus either as knowing the answers to his questions, or simply using his questions to test his disciples (cf. Jn. 6:5). This has prompted some commentators to suggest that as the early church developed and an increasing reverence for the divinity of Jesus, later narratives were unwilling to depict Jesus asking questions to which he did not know the answer. Certainly, in John's Gospel, it is notable that Jesus' questions are often presented as spiritually esoteric and quite difficult to interpret.

Types of Question

Before exploring the subject of Jesus' questions, it is useful, perhaps, to think a little about questions themselves.

Questions are linked to the verb 'to ask'. We *ask* questions, and the usual purpose is to elicit an answer. In the written text such questions are punctuated with a question mark. Slightly different is the occasion when one '*asks for*' something, e.g., *for* a glass of wine, or *for* an opinion. This is 'to request' or 'to enquire' rather than 'to question'.

Direct and Indirect Questions

Direct questions seek to gather information. Rudyard Kipling famously listed them as: -

I have six honest serving men
(They taught me all I knew);
Their names are What and Why and When
And How and Where and Who.

These questions cannot be answered by just 'Yes' or 'No'. They are often used, therefore, as a test of knowledge and form the root of examination questions or personal questions. Each question is designed to prompt a factual answer. What happened? Why did it happen? When, where, and when did it happen? Who was involved? The premise is that the person will think about their response and provide a quick short answer. Jesus often used such questions.

If the direct form of question sometimes seems unnecessarily brusque, the indirect form can be used. It sounds more formal or polite, e.g. "Please, will you tell me what happened?" "Can you explain why it happened?" "May I ask when it happened?" In English translations of the Gospels, the indirect question is a construction Jesus seems not to have used.

Open, Closed, and Tag-Questions.

Direct and indirect questions can also be described as open or closed.

The closed question often restricts the answer to 'Yes' or 'No', or a short quick phrase. Control of the conversation remains with the questioner. Jesus often used this form of a question. Closely associated is the 'tag question' such as 'isn't it?' or 'don't you?' or 'can't they?' When added to a statement it serves to convert it into a question, "It's great weather, isn't it?" "You always do this, don't you?" Jesus sometimes adopted this type of question, for example, "The wedding guests cannot fast while the bridegroom is with them, can they?" (Mk. 2:19).

The open question deliberately seeks a longer type of answer, often inviting an opinion or personal feelings. Control of the conversation then passes over to the respondent. Jesus did not often use the open question!

The Rhetorical Question

Not all questions demand an answer, and these are spoken of as 'rhetorical'. Really, they are statements taking the form of a question but only for effect. Their real purpose is not to obtain information. It is to persuade. The speaker neither awaits nor expects a reply. (The technique is not uncommon in sermons. "Some people snigger at scenes of the crucifixion. What do we do? Do we laugh? No! Do we cry? No! Do we complain? No! Do we marvel at their disrespect? No! And why? Because in our hearts we *know* that Jesus is the Christ. We can ignore them!") Plainly, the questions are not genuine. They do not seek answers. They are used simply to incite opinion and to prepare the ground for the point we want to make.

The rhetorical question was a form used frequently by Jesus.

The Question, 'Why?'

In addition to rhetorical questions, there are others that also might be called 'non-questions'. Some are simply unanswerable. "Mummy, are we having a good time yet?" Others are not answerable without clarification. "What do you think of his faith?" It all depends on what you mean by 'faith'. And then there is the question, 'Why?'

'Why is grass?' seems nonsensical. Nevertheless, it serves to remind us that the question 'Why?' really can be answered only in terms of two other questions;

in this case, 'How does grass come about?' and, 'For what purpose do we have grass?' In short, the question 'Why' usually embodies one question concerning the past and one concerning the future. We shall have cause to note this in several questions Jesus asked.

The Counter-Question

The counter-question refers to answering a question with a question. It is one of the oldest forms of argument. Often associated with appeals to scripture it is characteristic of rabbinical discourse. It was used often by Jesus as a form of defence or as a lead into a counterattack. In the modern age, it appears as a common form of political manoeuvring. The question, "Will you be raising taxes this year?" Answer, "What would you do if you were in my position?"

Leading and Assumptive Questions

Leading questions are phrased in a way that suggests what the answer should be. So, to ask, "What speed was the red car doing when it hit the blue car?" suggests that the red car was at fault. Alternatively, "What was the speed of the two cars when they collided?" does not. Assumptive questions are similar. They take some given situation for granted. Thus, "How much do you care?" assumes that you care. (The classical example is, "Have you stopped beating your wife?")

As we shall see several of Jesus questions are assumptive in that they take for granted certain beliefs of the day.

Special Questions. Apophthegms and *a fortiori* Arguments

Form criticism of the documents from which the Gospels are derived suggests that, in general, the shorter sayings of Jesus come down to us in one of two forms. 'Logions' are collections of isolated statements, or community rules, or prophetic utterances, which have no accompanying story. Other collections are called 'pronouncement stories' or apophthegms. Usually, they are found embodied in a miracle story or some other anecdote.

Examples associated with Jesus' discussions include his question concerning the forgiveness of sins (Mk. 2:5b–10a). This is inserted into the miracle story of the healing of the paralytic at Capernaum (Mk. 2:1–5a, 10b–12). Also, Jesus' question about the denarius (Mt. 22:19–21a). This is enclosed in the discourse on paying taxes to Caesar (Mt. 22:15–18, 21b). Questions of this type are often controversial questions that focus characteristically on such community issues as marriage, divorce, baptism, or working on the Sabbath.

A fortiori arguments are arguments from strength, arguments based on a strong proposition. Jesus often used a question as his strong proposition. Thus, in denouncing the hypocrisy of the Pharisees (Lk. 11:37–41) he asks, "Did not the one who made the outside make the inside also?" Or, in claiming that a house divided against itself cannot stand (Mk. 3:22–26) he asks, "How can Satan cast out Satan? If a kingdom is divided against itself that kingdom cannot stand."

In Closing

Undoubtedly, questions are revealing. They can be intelligent or fatuous and much can be learned from reflecting on who would ask such a question. Sometimes it can be asked only by a person who has 'inside' information, or who had thought about the issue, or who knew the people involved, or who had local knowledge of the place. Questions can be 'pointed' and specifically aimed. They can be 'dangerous' leading to fatal disclosures. They can be 'arrogant', 'impertinent', 'thoughtless' and 'insensitive'. And there can be questions left 'silent' because no one wishes the issue to be raised.

In exploring Jesus' questions, it becomes clear that he often used the direct question in its closed form. The rhetorical question and the counter-question were also characteristic of his Rabbinical style of teaching and frequently formed the basis for an argument *a fortiori*. It has to be acknowledged, however, that little is known of the nuances surrounding Jesus' questions; the inflection of his voice, his accompanying look, the attitude of his respondents, or the recent dialogues that shaped the construction of his question. We simply have to do the best with what we have.

Nevertheless, many of his questions might fairly be described by a wide spectrum of adjectives, such as 'challenging', 'persuasive', 'defensive' or sometimes, perhaps less happily as 'sorrowful', 'reproachful', and even 'despairing'.

How Jesus' questions arose, when and where they were asked, to whom they were addressed, the purpose in asking them, and how others have interpreted them are all matters to explore in the pages which follow. Hopefully, it is a study that will provide a glimpse into the wonder and mystery of Jesus' nature.

Mark's Gospel
1. Which Is Easier?

Jesus Heals a Paralytic at Capernaum, Mk. 2:1–12* (Mt. 9:1–8, Lk. 5:17–26)

According to Mark, Jesus was at his home in Capernaum with so many people gathered round about it that there was hardly room for them even in front of the door. Jesus, it seems, was speaking to them about God's purposes. Some people, some men, probably four of them, were trying to bring to Jesus to set before him a paralysed man lying on a mat. Finding no way to get near to Jesus because of the crowd the four men carried the paralytic up onto the roof of the house.

Palestinian dwellings usually had a flight of stone steps built on the outside of the house leading to a flat roof probably made of sticks and packed with earth. Once there, Mark tells us that the men removed part of the roof by digging through it. Matthew says they removed various tiles. Then, lowering the mat on which the paralysed man lay, the four let him down to the middle of the crowd in front of Jesus. When Jesus saw the faith of these men, and there is no reason to suspect that all of them were not included, he said to the paralytic, "Son, your sins are forgiven." (Personally, I like the Matthean version, "Take heart, son; your sins are forgiven.")

Now, it may have been Jesus' intention to convey to the man that in addition to his sins being forgiven he was cured physically also, although this is not clear from Jesus' words.** It is evident, however, that what Jesus actually said was not well received by some scribes sitting nearby and probably some Pharisees also. We are told that they questioned in their hearts how it came about that Jesus spoke in this way. To them, his words seemed blasphemous.

Only God could forgive sins and forgiveness was reserved for the time of future judgement. However, what probably disturbed his critics even more than his assumption of the divine prerogative was Jesus' authoritative manner. There was no suggestion here of him *praying* that the man's sins would be forgiven or *trusting* that they would be forgiven. His words were declaratory, "Son, your sins *are* forgiven!"

So, the scribes and Pharisees murmured quietly amongst themselves, and perhaps not without reason. It was easy to declare sins are forgiven when no one can prove otherwise. By contrast, to claim to be able to heal with a word could readily be tested.

Jesus, perceiving intuitively (i.e., 'in his spirit') the thoughts of his opponents, their murmurings and their unspoken challenge to his authority, immediately put this question to them.

"Why do you raise such questions in your hearts? Which is easier, to say to the paralytic, 'Your sins are forgiven,' or to say, 'Stand up and take your mat and walk'? But so that you may know that the Son of Man has authority on earth to forgive sins" – he said to the paralytic – "I say to you, stand up, take your mat and go to your home."

To the amazement of everyone, the man did so.

Jesus' question is rhetorical, and the answer is obvious, but it is significant for other reasons also. This was his first serious encounter with the scribes and Pharisees. He was aware of their intellectual attitude and the stance they took regarding the letter of the Law as against the spirit of the Law. It was this conservative, legalistic and dogmatic attitude to religion that was to make them his continual opponents.

So, on this occasion, Jesus enables his question to precipitate a 'sign' (a miracle) which, quite unhesitatingly, he uses to claim both authority and right as 'the Son of Man', a messianic title not without controversy. This was quite uncharacteristic of Jesus. His usual use of 'signs' was to reserve them to heal or relieve suffering where individual cases appeared. In general, they were acts of mercy and compassion that Jesus sought to keep out of the public domain (cf. the 'Messianic secret').

With this first question, however, Jesus does not miss the opportunity in front of his enemies to display his healing power, and especially to avow his divine authority.

*This narrative is thought to be an apophthegm, a composite passage in which the section containing Jesus' questions (5:b–10:a) has been inserted into the separate story of a healing miracle (1–5:a; 10:b–12).

**Jesus' immediate focus on the forgiveness of sins rather than on physical healing is, perhaps, strange to us. Implicitly it suggests a connection between sin and illness which was not unusual at that time.

2. A Tag-Question
Jesus' Disciples Omit Fasting, Mk. 2:18–20
(Mt. 9:14–17, Lk. 5:33–39)

Jesus and his disciples were dining in the house of Matthew. Luke's Gospel tells us that Matthew was giving a great banquet in his house for Jesus! Many people were there, and a large crowd of tax collectors and sinners were sitting at the table with Jesus and his disciples. When some Pharisees and scribes who were present saw what was happening, they questioned Jesus' disciples asking why he ate with such people.

In response to their open hostility and before his disciples could reply, Jesus answered almost in proverbial terms that people who were well had no need of a physician, only those who were sick. He then added that he had come to call to repentance not the righteous but sinners!

Amongst the other people who were present some had noticed that the Pharisees and the disciples of John the Baptist were fasting. * So, the people put a question to Jesus. (In Matthew, the question is phrased as having been asked by John's disciples themselves.)

"Why do John's disciples and the disciples of the Pharisees fast, but your disciples do not fast?" Jesus said to them, "The wedding guests cannot fast while the bridegroom is with them, can they? As long as they have the bridegroom with them, they cannot fast. The days will come when the bridegroom is taken away from them, and then they will fast on that day."

Jesus' response is interesting. Again, it is virtually a proverbial statement, but this time manipulated by the tag-question, *'can they?'* As a counter-question, it is leading, rhetorical and closed and the expected answer is obviously, 'No!' By its use, however, Jesus cleverly changes the subject. He directs it away from the principles of fasting and towards an understanding of his ministry. Plainly, it is a question he intends to answer himself.

While acknowledging implicitly the principle of fasting as a sign of repentance, Jesus makes clear that at present this does not fit the circumstances of his life and that of his disciples. Their association with him was an occasion for joy. It could be likened to a wedding feast. So, while fasting may be appropriate for some occasions it was entirely inappropriate for a joyous wedding celebration.

In answering his own question, Jesus also makes it implicitly clear that in speaking of 'the bridegroom' he is referring to himself. The Baptist's disciples would be particularly aware of this because John had previously referred to Jesus as 'the bridegroom' (Jn. 3:28–29).

Having defended his disciples by claiming that, as wedding guests, they are to be joyous for as long as he is with them Jesus then makes one of his earliest allusions to his death. He indicates that there will be time enough to fast when he is taken from them!

*Perhaps the disciples of John were fasting in response to their leader having recently been arrested and 'taken away' from them (Mk. 1:14). The Pharisees often fasted twice a week, on Monday and Thursday (Lk. 18:12). It was not obligatory. Jesus' disciples seemed to have no fixed rule regarding fasting.

----

3. Have You Never Read What David Did?

Jesus and the Sabbath Laws, Mk. 2:23–28
(Mt. 12:1–8, Lk. 6:1–5)

What is sometimes spoken of as 'the Sabbath battle' refers to several incidents wherein Jesus or his disciples were accused by their opponents of failing to observe the Sabbath as a day of rest. Jesus, it seems, quite often healed on the Sabbath and these occurrences include the exorcism of a man with an unclean spirit (Mk. 1:21f, 29–31), plucking grains of corn (see below), curing a man with a withered hand (Mk. 3:8–5), also a woman bent over and unable to stand upright (Lk. 13:10f), a man with dropsy (Lk. 14:1f), a lame man at Bethesda (Jn. 5:1f), and a blind man (Jn. 9:1f).

On the present occasion, which probably is the first of the Sabbath disputes (Matthew places it later than Mark and Luke) we are told that Jesus and his disciples were walking through a grain field. The disciples plucked some heads of grain and ate them, most likely after rubbing them in their hands. Apparently, some Pharisees who observed this criticised Jesus by asking him why his disciples were doing what was unlawful on the Sabbath. (In Luke, the Pharisees' question is directed at the disciples rather than at Jesus.)

Actually, what was regarded as unlawful on the Sabbath was putting the sickle to standing grain (Dt. 23:25). It was reaping that was prohibited not gleaning. On this occasion, the Pharisees obviously chose to regard the disciple's action as reaping and put their question. It is thought that only the more rigid Pharisees would regard the disciple's action of plucking corn as forbidden!

In each Gospel, it is Jesus who replies:

"Have you never read what David did, when he and his companions were hungry and in need of food? He entered the house of God, when Abiathar was high priest, and ate the bread of the Presence, which it is not lawful for any but the priests to eat, and he gave some to his companions." *

Had Jesus so wished he could have replied to the Pharisees simply by refuting their false accusation. He chose, however, to base his reply on a rhetorical counter-question followed immediately by a reference to scripture. This was a common form of rabbinical argument the usual purpose of which was to establish a notable exception to some general rule. In this instance, Jesus cites (1 Sam. 21:1–9), which evidently is one that people accepted as a competent authority.

The bread of the Presence, also known as Shew-bread, was twelve loaves in two rows of six each placed on a table daily in the sanctuary, the Holy place in the Temple (Lev. 24:5–9, Exod. 25:30). This bread could be eaten only after fresh loaves had replaced it. When David and his hungry men appeared, there was no food available other than the shew-bread. Jesus cites the case, therefore, to emphasise that sometimes physical needs can be more important than ritual laws.

Unexpectedly, Jesus' question on this occasion is inherently weak. The Pharisees were anxious to discover what exception Jesus could offer for his disciples' failure to observe the Sabbath as a day of rest. In reply, Jesus sought to claim that even on the Sabbath it was reasonable to gather food to feed people who were very hungry. In such circumstances, the act of meeting human needs equated to a lawful act on the Sabbath!

The weakness in this argument stems from the passage Jesus cited. In that narrative, David and his hungry men were given the consecrated bread by Ahimelech* but no mention is made either of the Sabbath or to a case of dire need. Nor indeed do the Gospel writers present Jesus' own disciples as being in any danger of starvation. Jesus' question, therefore, has little bearing on the issue raised by the Pharisees. Matthew appears to have recognised this weakness and adds a further scriptural reference (Num. 28:9–10) in support of Jesus' argument.

Whatever the inadequacy of the passage cited by Jesus, it clearly served to discomfort his opponents and sharply contrasted their narrow legalistic opinion against his own broad humanity.

*When David ate the consecrated bread, the priest was Ahimelech (1 Sam 21:1–6). Abiathar was the high priest during David's reign as king (2 Sam 15:35).

----

4. Is It Lawful?

Jesus Cures a Man with a Withered Hand.*
Mk. 3:1-5 (Mt. 12:9-14, Lk 6:6-11)

This narrative is the second of two in Mark's gospel relating to the Sabbath battle. It further illustrates the growing opposition of the authorities towards Jesus.

Jesus had entered the synagogue where there was a man who had a withered hand. Luke tells us it was the man's right hand. Under the watchful and hostile eye of the Pharisees, Jesus says to the man, "Come forward. Stretch out your hand." He stretched it out and his hand was restored. Matthew adds "as sound as the other."

Interestingly, Jesus did not touch this man. (Had he done so the more rigorous Pharisees may have interpreted this as 'work'.) No healing techniques were involved. Jesus simply commanded the man.

Within this miracle story is embodied a question which Jesus addresses to the Pharisees.

Then he said to them, "Is it lawful to do good or to do harm on the Sabbath, to save life or to kill?" But they were silent. He looked around at them with anger; he grieved at their hardness of heart...

In response to their silent criticism, Jesus' counter-question is open, direct, and penetrating. It went right to the heart of the matter. It was based on 'the omission principle', namely that when opportunity offers to do something good (i.e., beneficial), to *omit* to do it, even on the Sabbath, is tantamount to inflicting injury.

To let slip the chance, to withhold what good might be done, equates to causing harm! It was an argument against Pharisaic fundamentalism. Jesus was at pains to point out that it is the spirit of the Law, not the letter which must govern human lives.

Without the second part of his question, "to save life or to kill?" the first part, "Is it lawful to do good or to do harm on the Sabbath?" would have been merely a non-specific generalisation. By adding this qualification Jesus dramatically clarified his meaning. In effect, he questioned, "If, for legal reasons, one declines to save lives on the Sabbath does this amount to killing?" It is hardly surprising that the Pharisees remained silent.

Probably, most of them would have agreed with the generalisation that it was lawful to do good on the Sabbath and avert evil. Also, in more specific terms they would have acknowledged that a large number of illnesses might be attended on the Sabbath if they were dangerous. The fact remained, however, that this man's life was not in danger and his hand could have been attended to later. Plainly Jesus thought otherwise.

The context of Jesus' question suggests that this whole situation had much less to do with healing on the Sabbath and much more to do with the growing conflict between Jesus and the Pharisees. Outwardly Jesus' question seems direct and clear. We are told by Mark, however, that the Pharisees were seeking to accuse Jesus and questioned him silently.

Luke tells us that supernaturally Jesus knew what the Pharisees were thinking. Implicitly, therefore, Jesus' question throws out an unspoken challenge. "Who, truly, is breaking the Sabbath? Is it me because I perform a work of mercy, or is it you who seek to do me injury and even now plot my destruction?"

Although this implicit question was never voiced, it remained. Meanwhile, for the Pharisees the issue was clear. The Law regarded the Sabbath as a day of rest. Healing on the Sabbath was excusable only when life was endangered. To break the Sabbath otherwise was an offence punishable by death (Ex. 31:12-17). It was not inevitable that Jesus would heal the man but if he did, they might accuse him! So, they watched to see what Jesus would do. He simply ordered the man to stretch out his hand, and it was healed. What were they to make of that?

Mark reports that Jesus looked at his opponents and he was *angered* by their narrow vision of the Law. He *grieved* at their spiritual blindness, (their 'hardness of heart').

Matthew's narrative does not differ though he writes that the Pharisees *openly* asked Jesus if it was lawful to cure on the Sabbath. Jesus replies: -

"Suppose one of you has only one sheep and it falls into a pit on the Sabbath; will you not lay hold of it and lift it out?"

Again, the question plainly is rhetorical, and the obvious answer is, 'Yes'. There was general agreement that responding to unexpected accidents or danger on the Sabbath were acceptable exceptions to the rule. Chronic conditions, however, could wait until another time.

In these narratives, it is revealing how Jesus uses questions to uncover principles rather than rules. With penetrating clarity, he cleverly sets the broad principles of virtue and wickedness against the narrow legal rules of right and wrong.

*This passage has all the appearance of an apophthegm. There is a miracle story (vv. 1–3, 5b) into which has been introduced Jesus' question (vv. 4–5a) to make a combined narrative.

----

5. How Can Satan Cast out Satan?

The Beelzebub Controversy, Mk. 3:22–26
(Mt. 12:22–30, Lk 11:14–23)

In each of the first three Gospels, the context of the Beelzebub controversy is different. However, in each case the scene surrounding Jesus is charged with emotional activity.

In Matthew, following the healing of a man with a withered hand, we are told that many crowds followed Jesus all of whom he cured. The people brought to him a man believed to be possessed by a demon causing the sufferer to be both blind and dumb. Jesus cured the man. The Pharisees claimed it was only by Beelzebub* that Jesus cast out the demon.

In Luke, the man is described only as mute. The demon also is mute. As in Matthew, Luke tells us that Jesus cast out the demon and the man was cured so that he could see and speak. The people were amazed. Many cried that Jesus might be the Son of David. Others demanded that Jesus show them signs from heaven. Some shouted that he was casting out demons by Beelzebub.

In Mark, there is no mention of an exorcism. Rather, the Beelzebub controversy follows a great deal of activity in Capernaum after which Jesus returned home where a large crowd continued to press him. Indeed, such was the commotion surrounding Jesus' family that they could not even eat their meals. Mark suggests that they so feared for Jesus' sanity that they went out to bring him in because people were shouting, "He has gone out of his mind!" (Interestingly, there was another occasion also when the view was expressed that Jesus was possessed by a demon and out of his mind, John 8:48, 52, 10:19).

Mark records that amongst the crowd there were enemies of Jesus, scribes from Jerusalem. (Matthew speaks of Pharisees.) Possibly they had been sent by the authorities to report on Jesus' activities. Whatever the reason, these opponents, echoing a suggestion already voiced by some people in the crowd, now accused Jesus not only of being possessed by Beelzebub but also of casting out demons by this ruler of demons! "He has Beelzebub," they said, "and by the ruler of the demons he casts out demons."

We know that exorcism played a considerable part in Jesus' ministry. Frequently it caused amazement. Here the situation is different. In Mark's narrative, Jesus is accused of being *possessed* by Beelzebub. Naturally, Jesus denied this. The accusation was illogical. Beelzebub was normally hostile to humankind and now he is unexpectedly credited with curing the blind mute. On restoring some order to the situation, Jesus very sensibly asks:

"How can Satan cast out Satan? If a kingdom is divided against itself, that kingdom cannot stand. And if a house is divided against itself, that house will not be able to stand."

His question is assumptive. It not only assumes the reality of Satan but also equates Satan to the ruler of demons.** This, in turn, presupposes a two-kingdom theology, one ruled by God and the other by his adversary.

Rhetorically, Jesus' question leads directly into a typical *a fortiori* argument, (i.e., an argument from strength). *If* it makes no sense for a kingdom or a household to be divided against itself, *then* it makes no sense for Satan to antagonise the inhabitants of his own domain. *Therefore,* Satan does not 'cast out Satan' because to do so would simply lead to self-destruction.

Having revealed the misplaced logic of his adversaries, Matthew and Luke report that Jesus further challenged his critics with a probing counter-question. This again exposed the weakness of their argument. He asks:

"If I cast out demons by Beelzebub, by whom do your exorcists cast them out?"

Now his critics were faced with the question of whether they were going to make similar judgements on their own disciples. The obvious answer was, 'No!'

In each of the gospel narratives, underlying Jesus' questions is the argument that when demons are driven out of Satan's kingdom it is because they have encountered an external power greater than their own. In Mark and Luke, Jesus implicitly claims this greater power. In Matthew, he makes it explicit by a further question. He asks:

"How can one enter a strong man's house and plunder his goods, unless he first binds the strong man?"

Here Jesus acknowledges the strength of Satan. At the same time, he claims his own superior power to enter Satan's territory, curb his activity, and spoil his goods! Jesus always saw exorcism as part of the battle against Satan's kingdom.

*'Beelzebub', always in Greek manuscripts; 'Beelzebub' in the Latin Vulgate and others.

**'Satan', sometimes called the devil, cf. the temptation of Jesus, Mt. 4:1–11.

----

6. Who Are My Mother and My Brothers?
Jesus Questions His Family Relationships,
Mk. 3:32–33, (Mt. 12:46–50, Lk 8:19–21)

This narrative directly follows Mark's account of the Beelzebub controversy. Jesus' mother and his brothers had come out of their house to call him but could not reach him because of the crowd sitting about him to whom he was speaking. The people no longer seemed hostile and they told Jesus, "Your mother and your brothers and sisters are outside, asking for you." (Luke does not mention Jesus' sisters.)

And (Jesus) replied, "Who are my mother and my brothers?" And looking at those who sat around him, he said, "Here are my mother and my brothers! Whoever does the will of God is my brother and sister and mother."

(The parallel texts are very similar though again Luke omits 'sister'.)

Jesus' response is unexpected and, perhaps, startling. As he answers his own rhetorical question it seems almost as though he had experienced sudden self-realisation that his divine relationship to God now must take precedence over his relationship to his human family. It was not that he ceased to acknowledge his family, only that he realised that he could no longer be defined by his family constraints. His connection with his home could no longer be as it was. A new and more spiritual relationship had arisen, separating him from his mother, brothers and sisters.

It would hardly be surprising if his question was tinged with a note of both surprise and sadness.

----

7. Do You Understand This Parable?

The Parable of the Sower, Mk. 4:1–9, 13–20
(Mt. 13:3–9, 18–23, Lk. 8:5–8, 11–15)

Jesus was teaching a very large crowd by the sea of Galilee. He began with the parable of the Sower. * Later, the disciples asked Jesus about it and he began his explanation with two questions (only in Mark).

And he said to them, "Do you not understand this parable? Then how will you understand all parables?"

It remains uncertain amongst commentators whether this text should be treated as a question or simply as a statement. The difference seems hardly important. In either case, the text is revealing.

Jesus usually distinguished between the spiritual opportunities of his disciples and the opportunities of those who were not his close followers. To those 'outside' he spoke in parables in the hope that people would more easily comprehend. It was his view, however, that it had been given to his disciples to know the secrets of the Kingdom of God. His questions on this occasion, therefore, disclose not only his expectation regarding their understanding but equally some surprise at their lack of insight into a parable which he perceives as essentially simple.** One suspects that, to the uncertain disciples, Jesus' questions implied a reproach!

*A sower went out to sow. Some seed fell onto the path to be eaten by birds; some fell onto the stony ground to be scorched by the sun; some fell among thorns to be choked; and some fell on good soil, which grew to yield grain thirtyfold, sixtyfold, and a hundredfold.

**The seed is equivalent to 'the word'. Satan steals some. Some people receive it, but they quickly fall away under tribulation. Some people hear it, but cares or riches choke them. Some people hear it, and they bear fruit abundantly.

----

8. Is a Lamp Brought to Be put Under a Basket?

A Lesson from a Lamp, Mk 4:21–23 (Mt. 5:15–16, Lk. 8:16–18, 11, 33)

Following the parable of 'the Sower' Mark and Luke include a group of Jesus' cryptic sayings. It is not altogether clear to whom these are addressed. In Mark probably, it is the twelve and those who were around Jesus when he was alone (v 10). In Luke, it is the disciples as part of a great crowd. In Matthew, it is the disciples to whom Jesus was speaking about their witness during his sermon on the mount.

Because the context of these sayings is obscure it is not easy to interpret their purpose as part of Jesus' teaching. In Mark's gospel, the sequence opens with a question though what prompted Jesus to ask it remains unclear. He says:

"Is a lamp brought to be put under the bushel basket*, or under the bed, and not on the lampstand? For there is nothing hidden, except to be disclosed; nor is anything secret, except to come to light. Let anyone with ears to hear listen!"

Plainly the opening question is rhetorical, closed and leading. The expected answer is obviously, 'No!' No sensible person behaves in this way. A lamp is not brought to be hidden away. That is not what a lamp is for. When it is concealed, a lamp is of no use to anyone!

The connection between Jesus' opening question and his following explanatory statements is not obvious. Possibly, his first explanation suggests that the only reason a lamp might remain hidden is until someone uncovers it. Then it can be used to provide light, to remove darkness, and to render things visible and clear. Does this statement suggest, perhaps, that the presence of the Kingdom is likely to remain secret until someone uncovers it?

Jesus' second explanation similarly suggests that it is not in the nature of truth to be kept secret. Rather, it is the purpose of truth to make manifest whatever is the case. The only reason for the truth to remain hidden is because it has not yet been disclosed. Again, does this imply that one day the truth about the Kingdom will be brought into the light? Thereafter it will truly serve to state correctly whatever the case might be. It is not to be permanently concealed.

Matthew does not report all these statements. He simply uses the initial analogy of light to encourage the disciples to let their light shine before others. Luke tends to follow Mark, but where Mark suggests that light and truth may temporarily be hidden away, Luke's account omits the suggestion of secrecy and more positively assumes that all will become clear.

The uncertainty surrounding Jesus' question is frustrating not least because of his closing insistence upon the importance of hearing his words. It can only be conjectural, but one wonders here whether Jesus is indicating that he believed the time had come for him to be more positive in declaring the Gospel openly.

*A bushel basket was a good size bowl, or probably a metal tub, which held about sixteen pints.

----

9. With What Can We Compare the Kingdom of God?

The Parable of the Mustard Seed, Mk. 4:30–32 (Mt. 13:31–32, Lk. 13:18–19)

In Mark and Matthew, this parable is the second of two concerning God's kingdom. In Mark and Luke, the parable is introduced by a double question the parallelism of which is a typical device in rabbinical teaching.

(Jesus) also said, "With what can we compare the kingdom of God, or what parable will we use for it? It is like a mustard seed, which, when sown upon the ground, is the smallest of all the seeds on earth; yet when it is sown it grows up and becomes the greatest of all shrubs, and puts forth large branches so that the birds of the air can make nests in its shade."

The double question is assumptive. It assumes the existence of 'the kingdom'. Almost certainly Jesus' concept of this was of an everlasting domain, probably a universal domain, in which God as the divine Ruler exercised supreme power and whose word was law amongst humankind. It is implicit in the Lord's Prayer that 'the kingdom' was yet to come, at least in its perfection. On other occasions also, the language Jesus used to describe the coming of the kingdom is plainly eschatological and apocalyptic.

The extent to which Jesus held that in him God's kingdom on earth was, in some way, already a present and active reality remains open to debate. Certainly, in likening the kingdom to a tiny mustard seed, which once sown surprisingly becomes the greatest of shrubs or a great tree, it seems possible Jesus understood his messianic activity to be the small beginning of a great conclusion. No time scale is implicit in the parable; only the assurance that what now appears to be small and hidden will not remain so but will increase to become universal. It simply is not possible to judge the outcome of the kingdom from its earliest beginnings.

Jesus' opening question is broad and general. It could have been used to introduce many other parables concerning the kingdom.

----

10. Why Are You Afraid?

Jesus Calms the Storm, Mk 4:35–41
(Mt. 8:23–27, Lk. 8:22–25)

It was evening and Jesus and the disciples were together in a boat crossing the Sea of Galilee to the eastern shore. Jesus was asleep on a cushion in the stern. Mark tells us other boats were with them. Matthew and Luke do not mention these other boats and their presence has no obvious purpose in Mark. Suddenly, and unexpectedly, a great windstorm swept down the lake causing waves to beat into the disciples' boat and threatening to swamp them. *

We are not told what happened to the other boats but arguing from silence either they turned back, or struggled with the storm, or were lost. The disciples woke Jesus and said to him, "Teacher, do you not care that we are perishing?" Luke has, "Lord save us! We are perishing!" Jesus awoke, rebuked the wind, and said to the raging sea, "Peace! Be still!" The storm ceased and all became calm. Mark reports that Jesus then questioned his companions. In Matthew, although both questions are put it is prior to the stilling of the storm.

(Jesus) said to them, "Why are you afraid? Have you still no faith?"

In asking why the disciples are afraid what Jesus really is asking is how it could come about, after what he had already shown and taught them, that they failed to believe in the protecting hand of God. Surely, if they had begun to perceive Jesus as Messiah, then they could hardly believe that God would allow Jesus to perish in a storm! His presence was the assurance of keeping harm away. Jesus' question expresses surprise!

In fairness to the disciples, at this stage of their relationship to Jesus, their understanding of him was still imperfect. They had only a limited knowledge of his healing powers. They knew but little of his arguments with the Pharisees and his teaching by parables. Certainly, they had no experience of Jesus controlling the forces of nature. It seems not unreasonable, therefore, that they were frightened.

Jesus' second question suggests reproach. (Luke is not quite so sharp, and only the disciples' faith is questioned.) In effect, Jesus asks the disciples whether they are *not yet* able to rely upon their trust in God to safeguard them. "Have you *still* no faith?" Again, Jesus seems to express surprise.

It is not part of the present study to explore what sometimes are called Jesus' 'Nature miracles'. The point of interest lies in Jesus' timeless questions as they concern the frightening conditions described in the Synoptics. It is not difficult to sympathise with the disciples whose 'snowflakes of faith melted in the heat of adversity'. We can only imagine what their response to Jesus' questions might have been.

Understandably, the reaction of the disciples to Jesus' supernatural powers is overwhelming. Their fear gave way to amazement. They became filled with a sense of awe and said to one another, "Who then is this that even the wind and sea obey him?"

*Sudden squalls of considerable violence are said to be common in parts of the Sea of Galilee.

----

11. What Is Your Name?
The Legion of Demons, Mk 5:1–20
(Mt. 8:28–34, Lk. 8:26–39)

In both Mark and Luke, the detailed narrative of Jesus exorcising a legion of demons abounds with bizarre figures and extravagant features. It takes place in the country of the Gerasene opposite Galilee where Jesus had come by boat. It concerns a man thought to be possessed by an unclean spirit, or spirits.

The man had long-lived amidst the tombs and on the mountains and is described as wearing almost no clothes. He was so enormously strong that he regularly broke the chains and shackles with which people had often tried to restrain him. No one had the strength to subdue him and he was always howling and bruising himself.

Mark tells us that as Jesus stepped out of the boat, he was immediately met by this possessed man. Jesus at once said to the demon:

"Come out of the man, you unclean spirit!" Then Jesus asked him, "What is your name?" He replied, "My name is Legion; for we are many."

In this context, the name 'Legion' is significant. It reflects a Roman Legion, a large and irrepressible force of about 6000 front-line soldiers plus a similar number of auxiliaries. In the context of the biblical narrative, it expresses the magnitude of the conflict in which Jesus was now engaged.

There are some interesting differences in the narratives of Mark and Luke. In Mark, it is the unclean spirit to whom Jesus addresses his question. The reply, "*My* name is Legion; for *we* are many," expresses in the one name the multitude of these evil spirits.

In Mark's account, it also is notable that Jesus' question is asked *just after* the exorcism has begun. It would be believed at that time that this enabled Jesus to gain a distinct advantage over the demons in expelling them into a herd of swine feeding nearby. In ancient times, a person's name was believed to be part of them. It expressed who and what they were.

To give one's adversary your name was to give them power over you. To harm a person, it was necessary only to curse their name. Thus, the demons' answer would be held to increase Jesus' power to drive them out.

In Luke's narrative, Jesus' question is put *just prior* to the exorcism. Also, it is addressed directly to the possessed man himself who replies simply that his name is Legion. This too was held to be important in exorcism. It enabled the sufferer to remember something of their original identity and to realise that they were not identical with the evil powers that possessed them.

In both narratives, Jesus' question seeks information and is direct. Also, it is assumptive for it assumes a contemporary belief in possession by demons and the reality of a 'two-kingdom' theology. It is revealing too that in both Mark and Luke the demons are described as already having knowledge of Jesus as 'Son of the Most High God'.

This unexpected insight into the world of demonology reveals much about Jesus' perception of illness and his battle against the evil powers of Satan by exorcism.

----

12. Who Touched My Clothes?

The Woman with the Issue of Blood, Mk 5:25–34 (Mt. 9:20–22, Lk. 8:43–48)

The narratives in Mark and Luke describe a large crowd following and pressing about Jesus. Amongst them was a woman who despite spending all she had on seeking medical help was without benefit and had been suffering haemorrhages for twelve years. Whether her illness was intermittent or continuous is not indicated but the duration over twelve years is significant. Had her gynaecological condition been common knowledge almost certainly she would have been considered ceremonially unclean during this time (Lev. 15:25–30).

Mark tells us that the woman had heard about Jesus and presumably about his healings. Possibly her action was prompted by the ancient belief that supernatural cures sometimes were associated with the garments of famous healers, and sometimes even with their shadows*. Whatever the reason, "If I but touch his clothes" she said, "I will be made well."

So, believing that she might be cured independently of Jesus' will she came up behind him and touched his clothes. Matthew says it was the fringe of his cloak**. Mark and Luke report that her haemorrhage stopped at once. Mark adds that she felt in her body that she was healed of her disease.

Immediately aware that power had gone forth from him, Jesus turned about in the crowd and said, "Who touched my clothes?"

Both Mark and Luke report that Jesus realised within himself that power had flowed out from him. He turned, and despite the crowd pressing in on him looked about to see who was responsible. When the woman anxiously told him the truth, Jesus said to her, "Daughter, your faith has made you well; go in peace, and be healed of your disease."

The incident raises several points of interest regarding Jesus' healing ministry. For example, it is evident from his question that he was not consciously involved in the miracle as described by Mark and Luke. He did not know who

45

had touched him. He did not know who was cured. He was conscious only that power had flowed out of him.

How Mark and Luke gained insight into Jesus' private and personal awareness of this, or indeed into the suddenness of the woman's cure and her feelings, can only be speculative. The connection between the outflow of power and the cure also remains unclear. There is a degree of 'separateness', which suggests that Jesus did not always have supernatural knowledge of events surrounding him. Subsequently, he attributes the cure not to touching his clothes but to God's healing work in response to the woman's faith.

In Matthew's Gospel, where the account is slightly different, the connection between the outflow of power and the cure seems more apparent. It was only *after* Jesus turned and saw and spoke to the woman that she was made well.

*It is reported that God did extraordinary miracles through Paul. When the handkerchiefs or aprons that had touched his skin were brought to the sick, their diseases left them (Acts 19:12, c.f. also, Acts 5:15).

**The 'fringe' is thought to refer to four tassels of twisted blue threads at the lower hem of a square over-garment, one at each corner, two in front and two behind, sometimes worn by Rabbis (c.f. Numbers 15:38–40, Deut. 22:12). That Jesus wore this fringe indicates his observance of the Law.

----

13. Why Do You Make a Commotion?
The Raising of Jairus' Daughter, Mk 5:35–43
(Mt. 9:18–19, 23–26, Lk. 8:49–56)

In Mark and Luke, the context of this narrative is similar to that of the healing of the woman with the issue of blood. Jesus was by the sea and a great crowd had gathered about him. One of the leaders of the synagogue, whom Mark names as Jairus, came to Jesus and fell down before him in great distress*. Jairus thought his twelve-year-old daughter was at the point of death and he repeatedly begged Jesus to come and lay his hands upon her.

It was as they journeyed towards the leader's house that Jesus was delayed by his encounter with the woman who secretly had touched the hem of his cloak in the hope of being cured of her infirmity. Mark (v. 35) and Luke (v. 49) tell us that while Jesus was still speaking to her, messengers from the leader's house brought news that his daughter had died. There is a dreadful sense of finality in their news as they add, "Why trouble the teacher any further?" Plainly they thought it was too late for Jesus to be able to help.

Jesus, overhearing what they said, encouraged the leader not to fear but to hold faith. He then continued to the leader's house accompanied only by Peter, James, John, and the child's parents. They alone went in where they found professional mourners weeping and wailing loudly. Mark suggests the mourners were in an anteroom. Luke suggests they were in the room where the child lay.

And when (Jesus) had entered, he said to them, "Why do you make a commotion and weep? The child is not dead but sleeping."

Possibly because the mourners misunderstood his use of the word 'sleeping' they mocked Jesus and laughed at him. At this point, Mark reports that the mourners were dismissed and the five went into where the little girl lay. In Luke, it seems the mourners remained as witnesses to what followed.

Jesus took her by the hand and said, "Little girl, get up!" Mark tells us that she arose immediately and began to walk about. Luke's narrative records that

Jesus, compassionately and very practically, directs the people to give her something to eat!

Jesus' question plainly indicates a foreknowledge of the little girl's condition which he describes as 'not dead but sleeping'. How he knew this is unclear for he had neither seen nor examined her. Also, just what Jesus meant by 'sleeping' is ambiguous. Commentators point out that the word translated as 'sleeping' is the word used for natural sleep.

Nevertheless, the word is obviously used here to describe something more; indeed, something quite serious, possibly a coma resembling 'sleeping'. Jesus' action suggests far more than simply raising the child from a simple faint! It also is clear that whatever had caused the little girl's temporary loss of physical activity Jesus understood it to be something other than her final destruction. Thus, in saying to the girl, "Get up!" there is nothing to suggest that Jesus perceived his command as a form of resurrection to eternal life. Indeed, his subsequent direction to feed the little girl clearly emphasises her return to a normal earthly existence.

The puzzling features of Jesus' question include not only his foreknowledge and understanding of the girl's condition but also his unusual use of words.

*The context is different in Matthew's gospel. Jesus is at dinner with tax collectors and others when a leader of the synagogue came in and knelt before him. Otherwise, the narrative is similar, though less detailed and does not include Jesus' question.

----

14. How Many Loaves Have You?
Feeding the 5000, Mk. 6:34–44 (Mt. 14:14–21, Lk. 9:12–17, Jn. 6:1–13)

The narrative of Jesus feeding five thousand people is the only miracle to appear in all four gospels. * In Mark's narrative, the disciples asked whether Jesus wanted them to go and buy bread to feed such a large crowd. Presumably, their question expressed a degree of surprise.

And he said to them, "How many loaves have you? Go and see."

When they discovered they had only five loaves and two fish, Jesus took them and miraculously used them to feed everyone.

In John's narrative, a slightly different picture is presented. When Jesus saw a large crowd coming towards him, he anticipated that they would need to be fed and said to Phillip:

"Where are we to buy bread for these people to eat? He said this to test him, for he himself knew what he was going to do."

Quite clearly John writes as if he knew what was in Jesus' mind and that he put his question to Phillip only *to test him*. Otherwise, Jesus knew what he was going to do! Some commentators have suggested that the addition of this explanation was made by John in order to avoid presenting Jesus as not knowing the answer to his own question. In short, his question is simply rhetorical.

A similar approach has been taken by some about Mark's narrative. In order to avoid suggesting that Jesus did not know the answer to his own question, Mark adds, *"Go and see"*. Thus, instead of indicating ignorance on Jesus' part, the occasion becomes an exercise in trying to help the disciples understand who he truly is.

As it turned out we are told that the disciples did not understand the miracle of feeding the five thousand. They had been impressed by what Jesus had done but still had failed to recognise his divine nature (Mk. 6:51–52).

Perhaps the critique of these questions over-complicates the issue. Is it not reasonable to suppose that Jesus' questions simply emphasise some normal limitations on his life as 'truly human'?

*Two very similar variants are reported subsequently in Mk. 8:1–10, and Mt. 15:32–39.

----

15. Do You Also Fail to Understand?

Jesus Teaches on Defilement, Mk. 7:1–2, 14–15, 17–23 (Mt. 15:1–2, 5, 10–11, 15–20)

Mark's narrative tells us that Jesus and his disciples were in Gennesaret and that wherever he went crowds came to be healed by him. Some Pharisees and scribes also gathered about him. They had come from Jerusalem, perhaps to investigate Jesus' activities. On this occasion, they noticed that Jesus' disciples ate without first washing their hands.

So, they challenged him, "Why do your disciples not live according to the tradition of the elders, but eat with defiled hands?" They saw this omission not only as ceremonial and violating established tradition but also as rendering the disciples unfit to share in public worship. *

After Jesus had answered the first part of the Pharisees' question (c.f. Mt 15:1–9) he turned to the more immediate matter of unwashed hands. Calling the crowd to him he said, "Listen to me, all of you, and understand; there is nothing outside a person that by going in can defile, but the things that come out are what defile." This enigmatic saying would have both dismayed and angered Jesus' opponents as did his sense of authority.

For the Pharisees and scribes, it was a principle of Law that a number of physical conditions could make a person unfit to join in community worship. Particularly significant in this regard was the Mosaic distinction between clean and unclean meats. Jesus had disposed of this distinction and, as Mark adds later in parenthesis, "Thus he declared all foods clean."

Jesus then left the crowd and entered a house where his disciples asked him about his earlier saying regarding clean and unclean foods.

*He said to them, "Then do you also fail to understand? Do you not see that whatever goes into a person from outside cannot defile, since it enters, not the heart but the stomach, and goes out into the sewer? (Thus he declared all foods clean.)" And he said, "It is what comes out of a person that defiles. For it is from within, from the human heart, that evil intentions come."***

Jesus' challenging and critical question clearly denotes some frustration with both the crowd and his disciples. "Do *you also* fail to understand?" (Matthew has, "Are you also *still* without understanding?") Despite all that Jesus had tried to teach them did the disciples *not yet* understand?

Implicit in Jesus' question is his sense of expectation and disappointment. He had expected more of his disciples than of the crowd. He had expected his disciples to understand his challenge to Jewish regulations about food, to the whole concept of ceremonial pollution, and to the distinction between outward and inward religion. He had expected them to recognise his impatience with the narrow and unnecessary details of ceremonial ritual. He had expected them to understand that it was the spirit of the Law that mattered, not the letter!

If Jesus' disciples found his teaching difficult to grasp it seems hardly surprising. They were after all simple men for whom the traditional distinction between 'clean and unclean' had been ingrained since childhood. Clearly Jesus was still a riddle to them and his new attitude to the Law was not easy for them to understand. Perhaps the disappointment implicit in Jesus' question bespeaks an expectation the justification for which is open to question?

*To defile means to render unfit to share in public worship.

**In biblical Judaism, the anatomical basis for ethics is interesting. Here, the heart is depicted as the source of good and evil intentions.

----

16. Why Does This Generation Ask for a Sign?

The Pharisees Demand a Sign, Mk. 8:11–13
(Mt. 12:38–39, 16:1–4, Lk. 11:16, 29)

Immediately after the miracle of feeding four thousand people (c.f. Mk. 6:34–44) Jesus got into the boat with his disciples and sailed to the district of Dalmanutha (Magdala?) on the western shore of the Sea of Galilee.

In the district of Dalmanutha, the Pharisees came and began to argue with (Jesus), asking him for a sign from heaven, to test him. And he sighed deeply in his spirit and said, "Why does this generation ask for a sign? Truly I tell you, no sign will be given this generation." *

This was not the first time the Pharisees had sought to trap Jesus. On two previous occasions, they had been in dispute with him. One was at the healing of the paralytic at Capernaum when they tempted Jesus to display his miraculous healing power. The other was during the Beelzebub controversy when they charged Jesus with being possessed by the prince of demons in order to perform exorcisms.

Now, once again, the Pharisees argued with Jesus, this time asking him for a sign from heaven that would leave his claims in no doubt! It seemed to be their hope that if he refused to give a sign or attempted and failed, perhaps he would lose face before the people.

Not surprisingly Jesus sighed inwardly at the Pharisees' challenge, probably as much from irritation as frustration. His question, *"Why?"* characteristically rhetorical, asks first how it comes about that this generation still asks for a sign from heaven and then, secondly, what is the reason they ask for such a sign? In Jesus' view, for those who had eyes to see, the age was already full of signs and not least his own everyday ministry and that of John the Baptist. The reality was, however, that Jesus' opponents simply refused to believe his self-witness as the Son of Man.

So, they repeatedly asked for signs from heaven. Whether this was merely to satisfy their idle curiosity or, more significantly, to lay a trap for him was open to question. And what sort of sign could possibly convince them of the truth of his teaching? It might lead them to see him as a 'wonder man'. It would hardly convince them he was the Son of Man or increase their understanding of the kingdom.

When the right occasion demanded, Jesus did not hesitate to use his power to display his divine authority or to heal the sick. He always was unwilling, however, to use signs merely to prove himself and always refused to perform miracles just to satisfy the sceptical curiosity of his enemies. It was with authority, therefore, that he responded to his own question. "Truly, *I* tell you, no sign will be given to this generation." No sign would be given that was not already available to those who had eyes to see.

----

*Matthew speaks of this 'evil and adulterous generation'. Mark restricts his narrative specifically to the Pharisees as typifying a generation of Jews who rejected Jesus.

17. Why Are You Talking About Having No Bread?

The Yeast of the Pharisees, Mk. 8:17–21
(Mt. 16:5–12, Lk. 12:1)

Jesus had just finished an argument with the Pharisees who had asked him for a sign from heaven to test him. Jesus would give no sign, and with his disciples, he returned by boat to the eastern side of the Sea of Galilee. Mark reports that they had only one loaf in the boat and the disciples were expressing concern that they had forgotten to obtain sufficient bread.

Jesus, noting their anxiety then spoke to them in terms that they found strange. He warned them to 'beware of the yeast of the Pharisees and the yeast of Herod'. Commentators suggest that with this enigmatic passage Jesus sought to warn his companions to be heedful of Pharisaic hypocrisy and the 'irreligious worldliness' of Herod! In the minds of the disciples, however, there was no obvious connection between their immediate shortage of bread and Jesus' obscure reference to yeast. They simply misinterpreted his meaning and thought he was referring to their neglect in gathering sufficient bread.

And becoming aware of it, Jesus said to them, "Why are you talking about having no bread? Do you still not perceive or understand? Are your hearts hardened? Do you have eyes, and fail to see? Do you have ears, and fail to hear? And do you not remember? When I broke the five loaves for the five thousand, how many baskets full of broken pieces did you collect?" They said to him, "Twelve." "And the seven for the four thousand, how many baskets full of broken pieces did you collect?" And they said to him, "Seven" And he said to them, "Do you not yet understand?"

The strong rebuke in Jesus' multiple questions is revealing. As on a previous occasion, his questions charge the disciples with *still* not perceiving, *not yet* understanding, indeed with being *stupid.* (In context, 'hardening of the heart' can hardly mean 'wilful obstinacy'.) Have they learned nothing from all that they have been privileged to see and hear? How long is it going to take for them to grasp what he is trying to teach them?

Frustration, and even irritation, is mirrored in Jesus' every question. Has it not even occurred to them that if he could miraculously feed five thousand and four thousand people respectively with hardly any bread available, to worry now about one loaf was singularly foolish!

Jesus' questions are quite cutting. Perhaps they reflect a sense of urgency in seeking to awaken his disciples from spiritual dullness and a materialistic approach to his teaching.

----

18. Can You See Anything?

Jesus Heals a Blind Man at Bethsaida, Mk. 8:22–26 (Jn. 9:1–7)

Jesus and his disciples came to Bethsaida.

Some people brought a blind man to him and begged him to touch him. He took the blind man by the hand and led him out of the village; and when he had put saliva on his eyes and laid his hands on him, he asked him, "Can you see anything?" And the man looked up and said, "I can see people, but they look like trees walking." Then Jesus laid his hands on his eyes again, and he looked intently and his sight was restored.

As in the healing of the paralytic at Capernaum Mark emphasises the faith of others in bringing this blind man to Jesus. In this instance, the healing was a gradual process. It occurred in three stages, the application of saliva and the laying on of hands twice.

Jesus' question suggests that he was unsure what the effect of his initial attempt at healing would be. Possibly this was because he doubted the sufficiency of the man's faith. Alternatively, Jesus may have been uncertain what the effects of his saliva might be. (It is hard to imagine that he doubted the power in his own hands!)

Whatever the reason, when the man answered that he could see people, but they looked like trees walking it was obvious that something further was required in order to restore his sight fully. So, again Jesus laid his hands on the man's eyes and this time his sight was restored. He saw everything clearly.

Implicit in Jesus' question is the possibility that he did not always have complete foreknowledge of the effect of his miraculous power of healing.

----

19. Who Do People Say That I Am?

Peter's Confession on the Way to Caesarea Philippi, Mk. 8:27–29 (Mt. 16:13–16, Lk. 9:18–20)

Mark tells us that Jesus was travelling with his disciples to the villages of Caesarea Philippi. Matthew reports a similar setting. In Luke, the context is different and unclear, but the narrative is essentially the same.

On the way (Jesus) asked his disciples, "Who do people say that I am?" And they answered him, "John the Baptist; and others, Elijah; and still others, one of the prophets." He asked them, "But who do you say that I am?" Peter answered him, "You are the Messiah."

Jesus was approaching the end of his Galilean ministry. Soon it would be time to set his face towards Jerusalem and its inevitable consequences. Up to this point, Jesus' teaching had centred largely on the importance of the Kingdom of God, on encouraging his companions, and on the cost of discipleship.

Now, as his two questions clearly show, his focus transfers from the importance of his message to the significance of himself as a person. It was a defining moment both for him and for his disciples. Time was running out.

To what extent Jesus *expected* the replies he received remains open to question. Certainly, it was the first time he had addressed this matter so directly and openly. Whatever may have been his private self-realisation, when he put his first question it is difficult to imagine that he was completely unaware of what people said of him.

His healing ministry had brought him to the attention of many and he must have known what people murmured about him. His initial question, therefore, appears to have been deliberately designed to open a dialogue that would explore his self-designation as the Son of Man (cf. Mt. 16:13–16).

On this platform, Jesus raises his second question. It is, perhaps, tinged with a sense of hope that, unlike the crowds, his disciples had understood *at last* all he had tried to reveal to them? Often, they had misunderstood or misinterpreted what they had heard and witnessed. Nevertheless, they had always perceived in Jesus something that encouraged them to give up their normal way of life and follow him. An unspoken realisation and belief in whom Jesus was had been forming gradually in their minds.

Now, his question crystallised their understanding and for the first-time prompts Peter to articulate their conviction with a definitive answer, "You are the Messiah." Matthew has, "You are the Messiah, the Son of the living God." Luke has, "You are the Messiah of God."

It is notable that this conviction arose long *before* the disciples' experience of Jesus' crucifixion and resurrection. It also is interesting to note how Jesus uses his questions. Rather than instruct his disciples directly about his true status as the Christ, he prefers them to come to that belief themselves.

Perhaps there is no more profound question in the whole of the New Testament than Jesus' second question. It can be addressed to the twenty-first century just as it was to Peter.

----

20. What Can They Give in Return for Their Life?

Following Jesus, Mk. 8:34–37
(Mt. 16:24–28, Lk. 9:23–27. Cf. Mt. 10:38–39, Lk. 14:25, 17:33, Jn. 12:25)

In this part of Mark's Gospel, a sense of urgency prevails. The Day of the Lord was thought to be imminent. Time was short. The Kingdom and judgement were thought to be close. Jesus was teaching about the cost of discipleship and personal sacrifice. His emphasis lay on the importance of renouncing self-centredness and belonging to God. Calling to the crowd and those who would be his followers he said to them:

(34) *"If any want to become my followers, let them deny themselves and take up their cross and follow me. (35) For those who want to save their life will lose it, and those who lose their life for my sake, and the sake of the gospel, will save it. (36) For what will it profit them to gain the whole world and forfeit their life? (37) Indeed, what can they give in return for their life?"*

The apparent paradox in Jesus' opening argument (v. 35) rests upon two different meanings of the word 'life' (Gk *psuche**). In the first clause, it means 'bodily life'. In the second clause, it means 'the soul' or 'the self'. The premise of the argument, therefore, is that although people naturally want to preserve their physical existence (their 'bodily life') it is inevitable that a time will come when each person must die. However, if they are prepared to lose their soul for Jesus' sake, or for the good news he brings, their soul will be saved.**

Moving his argument forward (v. 36) Jesus then puts his first question. This reasons that there is no profit in seeking to gain the whole world (even if that was possible) if it is achieved at the expense of one's spiritual life hereafter. (In each of the Gospels, the same Greek word, *psuche*, is used and its meaning is the same.

However, perhaps it is best expressed in Luke which has, "What does it profit them if they gain the whole world, but lose or forfeit themselves?") It is a poor exchange to forego one's higher spiritual life in an effort to preserve bodily life merely to acquire earthly wealth. There is no adequate exchange for the soul. The value of the entire world is nothing compared to the value God sets on the soul of each person.

Jesus' second question (v. 37) is rhetorical but nonetheless dramatic. If one chooses to forfeit one's soul, how is one ever to recover it? There is nothing, even the whole world, which would enable one to retrieve it.

For his followers, Jesus' questions make clear his belief that death is not a loss but gain, and the gain of eternal life surpasses gaining all material things in this life.

*The New Testament has three Greek terms for 'life'.

Zoe. This is used most frequently. It denotes the total vitality of each and every living creature. However, in the context of humankind, it stands in sharp contrast to mere cellular existence and extends to the concept of eternal life shared, through Christ, with God.

Psuche. This term is difficult because it has a fluctuating meaning. Primarily it refers to the whole human being as an integrated combination of biological life with the full self-consciousness of body, soul, and spirit. This equates to "everything we are". Thus, in Mt. 20:28, we have "the Son of Man came not to be served but to serve, and to give his life (*psuche*) as a ransom for many," i.e., his whole being, his whole personhood, everything for which he existed on earth.

However, depending upon the context, *psuche* also slides easily between the animating principle of biological life and the subjective concept of soul or spiritual self.

Bios. This term is used only infrequently. In classical Greek its meaning is chiefly limited to the duration and biographical aspects of a person's present existence.

**Here, the two different ways in which Jesus uses the word 'life' is puzzling. It implies that the 'physical body' and the 'spiritual self' (soul) are separable. This concept resembles Greek philosophy. It is quite unlike the traditional Jewish view that the body and soul of a person are inseparable.

----

21. How Then Is It Written About the Son of Man?

Elijah Identified with John the Baptist, Mk. 9:9–13 (Mt. 17:1–13, Lk. 9:28–36)

In Mark's narrative of the Transfiguration (9:2–8), a vision is described in which Peter and James and John saw Jesus' clothes become dazzling white, and Elijah with Moses talking with Jesus. The disciples were frightened and became even more so when a cloud overshadowed them from which they heard a voice saying, "This is my Son, the Beloved, listen to him!" When they looked around, they saw no one, only Jesus.

As they came down from the mountain, they were ordered by Jesus to tell no one of what they had seen *"until after the Son of Man had risen from the dead."* Puzzled by this instruction they discussed between themselves what Jesus could have meant by it, for they found it difficult to associate their understanding of resurrection and their understanding of the Son of Man. This discussion is omitted by Matthew. Luke omits the whole section but reveals knowledge of it.

The disciples then asked Jesus:

[11]*"Why do the scribes say that Elijah must come first?"* [12]*He said to them "Elijah is indeed coming first to restore all things. How then is it written about the Son of Man, that he is to go through many sufferings and be treated with contempt?* [13]*But I tell you that Elijah has come, and they did to him whatever they pleased, as it is written about him."*

This passage is difficult to interpret. Commentators have suggested various rearrangements of the verses, but none has been entirely satisfactory.

Based on scripture (Mal 4:4–5) the disciples believed that at some future time prior to the Day of the LORD the prophet Elijah would appear not as a vision but as a person, a forerunner to usher in the Messianic age. It was their belief also that Jesus was Messiah (Mk. 8:9) a belief strengthened by the events surrounding

Jesus' recent transfiguration. What the disciples could not understand, therefore, and questioned Jesus about it, was why the scribes had said, "Elijah must come first" when that had not happened!

Jesus' reply is open to at least two interpretations. Perhaps the one most widely accepted is as a statement. Jesus agrees with the prediction of the scribes that Elijah must come first (12a) and goes on to state that indeed Elijah has come (13a).

Here, the broad implication is that John the Baptist is to be identified with Elijah, though this is far from clear in the text (cf. Mt 11:13–14, Lk 1:17). The next part (13b) also is obscure. It has been suggested that this is an oblique reference to the Baptist's life being threatened by Queen Herodias, as Elijah's life was threatened by Queen Jezebel (1 Kg. 19:2, 10).

An alternative interpretation regards the whole of v. 12 as a question indicating that the scribes were mistaken in their prediction about Elijah. "*If* Elijah is indeed coming first to restore all things, *then* how is it written etc.?*" In other words, because the scriptures *after* Elijah all include the sufferings of the Son of Man, it cannot be right that Elijah did 'restore all things' *in preparation* for the coming of Messiah.

Undoubtedly, Jesus' counter-question (12b) is placed awkwardly within the text. It interrupts his initial reply and abruptly changes the subject, moving the focus from the coming of Elijah to the role of the 'suffering servant' and the future of the Son of Man (c.f. Isa 53 and similar). As this is the only place in Mark's Gospel where Jesus' sufferings are said to be in accordance with scripture it strongly suggests, together with Jesus' earlier warning to the disciples, that this important matter was uppermost in Jesus' mind at the time.

Despite the difficulties with this text, it is interesting to note Jesus' characteristic use of the counter-question to re-direct discussion towards the important point.

----

22. What Are You Arguing About?

An Epileptic Boy Healed, Mk. 9:14–29
(Mt. 17:14–21, Lk. 9:37–42)

Following the narrative of the transfiguration, Mark reports that Jesus together with Peter and James and John returned from the mountain. "When they came to the disciples, they saw a great crowd around them, and some scribes arguing with them." Whether the argument included the disciples is unclear.

When the whole crowd saw (Jesus) – they ran forward to greet him. He asked them, "What are you arguing about with them?"

The reply revealed that, in the hope of seeing Jesus, an anxious father had brought his son believing him to be possessed by a troublesome spirit which caused him to be ill. The signs of the illness resembled epilepsy. When Jesus could not be found, the father had asked Jesus' disciples to cast out the spirit, but they could not. Whether this was the cause of the argument amongst the scribes and the people is not known.

Jesus answered them:

"You faithless generation, how much longer must I be among you? How much longer must I put up with you? Bring him to me." (The boy was brought and immediately had a convulsion.) Jesus asked the father, "How long has this been happening to him?" *

Following the subsequent dialogue, Jesus exorcised the spirit, and the boy was healed.

Jesus' first and last questions are straightforward requests for information. They make plain that he had no supernatural foreknowledge of the local situation.

His two rhetorical questions are more puzzling. It is difficult to imagine, for example, that Jesus would speak so directly to his disciples especially with scribes present. Probably, therefore, both questions were addressed to the crowd in general including the disciples and scribes, voicing an overwhelming and intolerable weariness even exasperation with his contemporaries as an unbelieving generation.

The two sorts of questions seem to reflect Jesus' status as both 'true man' and 'true God'.

*(Matthew and Luke have, *"You faithless and perverse generation".*)

----

23. What Were You Arguing About?
True Greatness, Mk. 9:33–37
(Mt. 18:1–5, Lk. 9:46–48)

Following the healing of an epileptic boy, Jesus and his disciples continued their journey through Galilee. As they travelled Jesus taught his companions and foretold them of the Passion. They did not understand and were afraid to ask him.

Then they came to Capernaum; and when he was in the house he asked them, "What were you arguing about on the way?"

Jesus' question makes clear that somehow, he had become aware of the disciples' argument if not its content. Luke says that Jesus knew *intuitively* what they had been discussing.

Mark and Luke explain that the disciples had argued with one another about who was the greatest, presumably thinking about precedence in the future Kingdom. Matthew reports that the disciples came to Jesus and asked, "Who is the greatest in the Kingdom of Heaven?"

Jesus's question was met with silence. Perhaps the disciples had learned how he would view such disputes. Possibly they were ashamed.

When no answer was forthcoming, Jesus did not chide the disciples but, using his question as a springboard, called them together to teach them that true greatness lies in being the servant of all.

----

24. How Can You Season It?
On Discipleship, Mk. 9:49–50
(Mt. 5:13, Lk. 14:34–35)

The setting for this narrative is slightly different in each of the three Gospels. In Mark, Jesus is teaching his disciples privately about the demanding conditions of discipleship. He has just emphasised the value of even the smallest kindness when it is shown to someone in Christ's name. Anything that impedes or devalues such an action is to be condemned. The disciples must learn the importance of discarding anything that may cause them to stumble as they strive towards the kingdom, even when this involves personal painful sacrifice. He then concludes by telling them:

"For everyone will be salted with fire. Salt is good; but if salt has lost its saltiness, how can you season it? Have salt in yourselves, and be at peace with one another."

Here, 'salt' is presented as a *purifying* agent, like fire. It is a good thing, and it symbolises what Jesus expects his disciples *to be*. His question then warns against salt losing its essential property and he reinforces his message with a supplementary lesson. Perhaps Jesus had in mind the disciples' recent discussion amongst themselves regarding who will be the greatest in the future kingdom (v. 34). That was the way to lose their 'salt'. To retain it they had to have confidence in themselves as disciples and peacefully support each other in their own distinctive ministry.

In Luke's gospel, Jesus' question is directed towards the large crowds that were following him.

In Matthew, Jesus' question is addressed to the disciples as part of his Sermon on the Mount. He is teaching them about the blessing God extends to those who live according to his rules. He tells them that 'salt' is what *they are*, and the context indicates salt as a *preserving* agent.

Plainly, just how Jesus expected his disciples to serve as 'salt' in the community is governed by the context of the different narratives. All three gospels, however, imply an experience, presumably common to Galileans, that it was possible for saline deposits from the dead Sea to have the salt-washed out of them leaving only *the appearance* of salt. In each narrative, therefore, Jesus' point is the same. Salt in name only is useless. Its saltiness cannot be regained!

The main message seems to be that as witnesses to 'the good news' it is important for the disciples to retain their self-dedication and not to lose heart or courage.

----

25. What Did Moses Command You?
On Divorce, Mk. 10:1–12 (Mt. 19:1–12, Lk. 16:18)

The scene of this narrative is not unfamiliar. Jesus was in the region of Judea and crowds again gathered around him.

Some Pharisees came, and to test him they asked, "Is it lawful for a man to divorce his wife?" He answered them, "What did Moses command you?"

The Pharisees' question is a controversial question. Some texts suggest it was the people who asked.

At the time of Jesus, there was a sharp division between the opinions of the Greco-Roman world and the orthodox Jewish community regarding divorce. Clearly, the question put to Jesus is hostile. It sought to bring Jesus into conflict with the vexed matter of interpreting Mosaic Law and it was put 'to test him'. Probably the situation implies, as commentators suggest, that Jesus' views on the issue of divorce were known to be distinctive and veered towards the teaching of Malachi (2:14–16), namely that God hated divorce and demanded marital fidelity.

Actually, the Mosaic Law provided no definitive answer to the Pharisees' question. The traditional Jewish view was modelled on the text in Deuteronomy (24:1–4) and held that the only form of divorce recognised was that of a wife by her husband. The initiative rested solely with him.

Given that he satisfactorily completed a certificate stating the grounds, divorce was legally permissible. There were, however, two schools of rabbinic thought that complicated this matter. Shammai was stringent in its interpretation. Hillel was more liberal. In neither school were the wife's interests seriously considered!

Jesus' counter-question opens the way to a complex of underlying issues. Acknowledging immediately that the question put to him is primarily a matter of Law he asks the Pharisees to state openly what the Law is! They reply in terms of the *Mosaic* Law (implicitly Deuteronomy 24:1–3) which Jesus does not question. He challenges their answer, however, on the grounds that this was written solely as a concession to meet the contingencies of an earlier time.

Since then the matter of divorce has assumed greater importance. Therefore, it is necessary to think again about how best to judge the grounds for divorce. To this end and referring to the narratives in Genesis of God's creation of man and woman, Jesus then argues that the divine sanctity of marriage is indissoluble in God's sight. The argument is not legal, but in Jesus' view, the *spirit* of God's law outweighs the *letter* of Mosaic Law!

One might readily suppose that Jesus' leading question anticipated the Pharisee's reply. Certainly, it opened the way for him not only to claim the right to interpret the Mosaic Law but also to go some way towards redressing the balance for disadvantaged women.

----

26. Why Do You Call Me Good?

The Rich Man, Mk. 10:17–22
(Mt. 19:16–22, Lk. 18:18–23)

Mark tells us that Jesus was just leaving the house in which he had been teaching his disciples and blessing children that people brought to him.

As he was setting out on a journey, a man ran up and knelt before him, and asked him, "Good Teacher, what must I do to inherit eternal life?" Jesus said to him, "Why do you call me good? No one is good but God alone."

The scene presents a rare picture of effusive oriental flattery. Mark recounts that the man, a 'youth' in Matthew, a 'ruler' in Luke, had many possessions. We are not told how old he was but the description that he came running to Jesus, knelt before him like a suppliant and addressed him with the extraordinary title 'Good Teacher' suggests one who was relatively young and successful.

His question is unusual and naive. His hope is to inherit 'eternal life', which in this context refers not to securing immortality but to entering the Kingdom of Heaven. It also is plain that he imagines this to be something he can achieve by what he *does*. It seems not to have occurred to him that eternal life is only ever a gift from God at the resurrection.

In the subsequent discussion, Mark tells us that when the young man claimed not to have broken any of the commandments since his youth, Jesus, looking at the man, loved him. Perhaps it was his impulsive enthusiasm that endeared him to Jesus. However, the man had yet to learn that his salvation did not depend on all the sins he had not committed.

Simply abiding by the rules was no more than negative goodness. Blamelessness was not enough. Entry to the eternal life of the Kingdom necessitated loving positively. That was the condition of discipleship.

Jesus' question suggests that he was discomforted by the man's approach. Jesus did not welcome flattery or false servility. Clearly also, in elaborating his question with the statement "No one is good but God alone," Jesus thought it necessary to distinguish between any goodness of his own, limited perhaps by his incarnation, and the absolute goodness of God.

Nevertheless, Jesus' question was hardly a rebuke. Rather it was a gentle reproach to one who yet needed to reflect on the use of such incautious language as, 'Good Teacher!'

---

27. What Is It You Want Me to Do for You?

Positions of Honour, Mk. 10:36–38
(Mt. 20:20–28, Lk. 22:24–27)

The narrative of this event is not dissimilar to an earlier dispute amongst the disciples regarding who might be the greatest in the Kingdom of Heaven, (Mk. 9:33–37 and parallels.) On the present occasion, Mark and Matthew place Jesus on the road going to Jerusalem. The setting in Luke is much later, on the occasion of the last supper. Despite the dreadful prospect that awaited him Jesus was resolutely walking ahead of his disciples who followed amazed and fearful. Jesus again took them aside and began to tell them that at Jerusalem he would be arrested, reviled, executed and, after three days, would rise again (cf. Mk. 8:31).

James and John, the sons of Zebedee, came forward to him and said to him, "Teacher, we want you to do for us whatever we ask of you." And he said to them, "What is it you want me to do for you?"

They wanted Jesus *to grant* them to sit at his right and left hand in his glory. (In Matthew, it is the mother of James and John who, kneeling before Jesus, asks a favour of him. She wanted Jesus *to declare* that her two sons would sit at Jesus' right and left hand in the Messianic kingdom.)

Jesus said to them, "You do not know what you are asking. Are you able to drink of the cup that I drink, or be baptized with the baptism that I am baptized with?"

This reference to baptism is somewhat obscure in Mark and is omitted in Matthew. Nevertheless, whereas Jesus' first question is quite ordinary this second one is not so.

In the context of Mark's narrative, it is difficult to imagine how the disciples' initial request ever came to arise. It hardly seems to connect with the disciples following Jesus in fear and amazement along the road to Jerusalem. Plainly James and John were more concerned with thoughts of glory and positions of honour when Jesus came to his throne in heaven. Moreover, they had completely failed to comprehend Jesus' explanation of the sacrifice incurred.

In response to their request, Jesus' second question is extraordinary. Clearly, it reveals his anticipation of forthcoming events if not direct foreknowledge. Using vivid metaphors which include the cup of suffering and baptism of death it is tinged with implicit drama. What state of mind accompanied this dreadful prospect can barely be imagined.

---

28. What Did You Want Me to Do for You?
Blind Bartimaeus, Mk. 10:46–52
(Mt. 20:29–34, Lk. 18:35–43)

In a vivid and descriptive narrative, Mark reports that Jesus and his disciples were travelling the road to Jerusalem and were now about fifteen miles southeast of the city.

As he and his disciples and a large crowd were leaving Jericho, Bartimaeus son of Timaeus, a blind beggar, was sitting by the roadside. When he heard that it was Jesus of Nazareth, he began to shout and say, "Jesus, Son of David, have mercy on me!"

Whether Bartimaeus shouting aloud in public, 'Jesus, Son of David' influenced Jesus' subsequent question is not clear. This was a Messianic title closely identified with the national hope for the return of a Davidic king. To shout it aloud was a dangerous thing to do politically. Potentially, on this occasion, it also implicated Jesus as King of the Jews. Not surprisingly, therefore, many in the crowd sternly warned Bartimaeus to be quiet but to no avail. (In Matthew's narrative, which otherwise closely follows Mark, there are two blind men calling out.)

Jesus called for Bartimaeus to be brought to him.

Then Jesus said to him, "What do you want me to do for you?"

Perhaps the question seems strange for it was obvious that the man was blind. His initial cry, however, had been only a non-specific generalisation, *"have mercy on me!"* Jesus' question, therefore, is essentially direct and requires the man to express his need more specifically. Whatever Jesus may have suspected, there is no suggestion here that he had any supernatural foreknowledge of the man's particular wishes.

Bartimaeus wanted to see again. Impressed with the man's faith Jesus simply declared that Bartimaeus would be made well and immediately his sight was restored. No healing action is described by Mark. The healing power of Jesus' declaration was sufficient. Luke also recounts that Jesus *commanded* the man's sight be received! Matthew, by contrast, tells us that in pity Jesus *touched* the eyes of the two blind men.

Jesus' question is simple but startling, a timely reminder perhaps of the importance of being specific in requests that we bring to him.

----

29. Is It Not Written?

Jesus Defends Cleansing the Temple, Mk 11:15–17 (Mt. 21:10–13, Lk. 19:45–46, Jn. 2:13–16)

In Mark's Gospel, the account of Jesus cleansing the Temple has much of the appearance of an apophthegm, i.e., it occurs within the separate narrative of Jesus' curse upon a fig tree (Mk. 11:12–14, 20–21).

The context of Jesus' question is important. It arises in the outer court of Herod's Temple known as the Court of the Gentiles. This was an area of approximately 26 acres surrounded by tall Temple walls. In the northern half of this great enclosure stood the Sanctuary surrounded by a low balustrade bearing the wording, "Foreigner! Do not enter within the grille and partition surrounding the Temple. He who is caught will have only himself to blame for his death which will follow."

Within the Court of Gentiles, it had become the custom for traders of all kinds to sell animals and doves for sacrifice; also, oil, wine, incense, and salt. Some traders, the 'money-changers', made a profit by exchanging Roman or Greek money from visiting pilgrims for the Jewish shekels required to buy Temple commodities. In practice, therefore, the Temple precincts had become largely an oriental market under the jurisdiction of the Temple police and the priests who turned a blind eye to its activities.

Mark tells us that Jesus had visited the temple after his triumphal entry into Jerusalem on Palm Sunday. Thereafter he retired to Bethany but returned to the Temple the following day. In view of the subsequent events, it seems probable that Jesus had been reflecting on what he had seen. Certainly, on the occasion of his second visit, it is clear he had decided to denounce what he saw as misuse of the Temple precincts.

After driving out those that were selling and buying:

Jesus was teaching and saying, "Is it not written, 'My house shall be called a house of prayer for all the nations'? But you have made it a den of robbers."

The basis of Jesus' question is of interest. It is a slightly altered quote from Isaiah 56:7 in which the prophet speaks of 'all peoples'. Here, Jesus adapts it to 'all the nations'. The original passage is part of a blessing on all who keep the Sabbath. It includes *foreigners* who align themselves to Yahweh, love him and wish to serve him.

The question, which appears only in Mark, could equally well have been presented as a statement with the addition of a tag question, "It is written – *isn't it?*" And similarly, "But you have made it etc. – *haven't you?*" In whichever form, the question rings with moral authority. Ostensibly it is addressed only to the crowd in general. Implicitly it is directed also towards the Sadducees and the authorities responsible for Temple activities. The rebuke is a direct challenge to their vested interests!

The rebuke Jesus offers following his question is rather unexpected. It is cited from Jeremiah 7:11 where the prophet proclaims that there is a need for a moral change in people of poor moral character who use the Temple merely as a place of refuge. Thereby they desecrate the Temple and reduce it to a den of robbers! The traders, however, under the rules governing Temple activities would certainly have considered their business to be legitimate.

Of course, their intention was to make a profit, but it remains open to question whether they were cheating! Nevertheless, Jesus' rebuke does seem to be directed towards the moral character of those buying and selling together with the impact that this might have upon the use of the Temple.

We know that from an early age Jesus had viewed the Temple as a place of instruction (Lk. 2:46). He referred to it as 'my Father's house' (Lk. 2:49) and now he refers to it as 'a house of prayer'. His question, therefore, seems designed towards re-establishing the instructional and prayerful nature of the Temple. It may even hold an implicit assertion of his own messianic authority as central to this.

Jesus' use of scripture in the form of a rhetorical question and his sense of authority in interpreting scripture are notable features of his teaching ministry. He frequently used both in order to defend his actions and defeat his opponents.

----

30. Did the Baptism of John Come from Heaven?

By What Authority? Mk. 11:27-33
(Mt. 21:23-27, Lk. 20:1-8)

This narrative appears to be a further example of an apophthegm set within a separate account of Jesus teaching his disciples on prayer and parables (Mk. 11:20–25 12:f).

Following the incident of driving the traders from the Court of Gentiles and leaving the crowd spellbound by his teaching, Jesus was again in Jerusalem walking and teaching in the Temple. Representatives of the Sanhedrin, that is the chief priests, scribes, and elders who were the ruling body in Israel, approached Jesus and asked him, "By what authority are you doing these things? Who gave you this authority to do them?"

Their question is reasonable if also a little aggressive. The members of the Sanhedrin were responsible for public order. Jesus was not an ordained rabbi. They felt entitled, therefore, to enquire on what grounds Jesus claimed authority for himself or from whom he had received it. Undoubtedly, when they spoke of 'these things' they had in mind not only Jesus' recent cleansing of the Temple and his powerful teaching but also his healings (Mt. 21:12, 14, Mk. 3:22–26).

Jesus said to them, "I will ask you one question; answer me, and I will tell you by what authority I do these things. Did the baptism of John come from heaven, or was it of human origin? Answer me."

In this narrative much rests on the word translated as 'authority'. In New Testament Greek, the word usually signifies divine or prophetic authority rather than legal right or political power. As used here by the representatives of the Sanhedrin it probably emphasises rabbinical authority. Jesus appears to have interpreted it more as divine authority.

As on several previous occasions, Jesus characteristically opens his defence with a challenging counter-question, an accepted form of argument in a rabbinical discussion. Plainly his question is not seeking information. Nor is it simply a more difficult question delivered on a 'knock for knock' basis. Rather, it seeks to establish whether Jesus and his opponents were using the same standard to judge the matter of divine authority.

In other words, by what criteria was a divine authority to be judged? Did it accrue solely from external rites of ordination or from an inward call the fruits of which are evident to all?

Neither John nor Jesus had ever claimed any external warrant for their authority. Nevertheless, the people acknowledged both as prophets because they had restored vitality to a religion that had become narrow and lifeless and was legalistically dominated by the letter of the Law.

So, the point at issue was startlingly clear. John had baptised Jesus and witnessed to his nature as the Son of God (Mk. 1:9–11, Jn. 1:34). Jesus was well aware that the people regarded John as a prophet sent from God. Indirectly, therefore, Jesus' question also referred to his own divine authority. If the Sanhedrin conceded John's divine authority, then they also conceded Jesus Messianic status!

The priests and elders found themselves in a dilemma. If they answered, "From heaven," Jesus could challenge them with, "Then why did you not believe him?" If they answered, "Of human origin," the crowd would be angry. So, they answered, "We do not know", to which Jesus' reply was almost scathing, "Neither will I tell you by what authority I am doing these things." In effect, he told them that he was not prepared to waste his time debating when nothing he said was likely to convince them.

Jesus' question is clever. His clear demand for an answer carries with it the strong implication that divine authority lies with him!

----

31. What Will the Owner of the Vineyard Do?

The Parable of the Vineyard, Mk. 12:1–12 (Mt. 21:(28–32), 33–46, Lk. 20:9–19)

In the synoptic gospels, the parable of the vineyard is preceded by the incident of Jesus cleansing the Temple and a discussion on authority with the representatives of the Sanhedrin.

In Mark, Jesus addresses his parable to all those surrounding him in the Temple and notably to the chief priests and elders who recently sought to arrest him. The basis of his parable is probably 'the Song of the Vineyard' (Isa. 5:1–7). This Old Testament passage is aimed at Jewish leaders who were expected to nurture the people of Judah but failed to do so and which resulted in dire consequences at the hand of Yahweh.

As told by Jesus the parable of the vineyard describes how a man planted it and left it in the care of tenants. Over a long period of time, the owner repeatedly sent his slaves to collect his share of the produce, but the tenants ill-treated each of them in turn. When, eventually, the owner sent his beloved son the tenants seized and killed him believing that thereby they would inherit the vineyard.

Although there is debate amongst commentators about the nature of this narrative, there is general agreement that the owner of the vineyard represents God, Israel is the vineyard, the Jewish leaders are the tenants, and the owner's beloved son is Jesus. The main thrust of the parable is to draw attention to God's long patience with Israel's leaders and to the ultimate inevitability of God's Justice. Whether Jesus anticipates his own passion in this parable is unclear.

Jesus puts two questions.

"What then will the owner of the vineyard do? He will come and destroy the tenants and give the vineyard to others. Have you not read this scripture; 'The stone that the builders rejected has become the cornerstone; this was the Lord's doing, and it is amazing in our eyes'?"

His first question is rhetorical, and Jesus answers it himself. In Matthew, the reply is made by the chief priest and the elders who thereby incriminate themselves. In Luke, the response of the people is, 'Heaven forbid'! The idea of Israel possibly being given to the gentiles is unthinkable!

The scripture Jesus cites in his second question is from Psalm 118:22–23. To this, he adds (Mt. 21:43) *"Therefore I tell you, the kingdom of God will be taken away from you and given to a people that produces the fruits of the kingdom."* Also, (Lk. 20:18, Mt. 21:44) *"Everyone who falls on that stone will be broken to pieces; and it will crush anyone on whom it falls"* (Isa. 8:14–15, Dan. 2:34–35, 44).

Jesus' appeal to these Old Testament passages seems to be to emphasise that the people who fail to recognise his messianic status will be subject to God's effective judgement!

In Matthew's gospel, just prior to the parable of the Vineyard, an additional parable is added the thrust of which is very similar. It concerns a man's two sons one of whom at first refused to obey his father but did so subsequently. The other said that he would obey but did not. Jesus then asks the chief priest and the elders:

"What do you think? Which of the two did the will of his father?"

They replied, "The first." Jesus then drives home his message. The tax collectors and prostitutes who changed their mind because they believed John the Baptist will enter the Kingdom of heaven before the rulers and the elders of the people. The authorities, despite all the evidence, failed to accept or acknowledge the righteousness of John. It is a stark reminder to the people to dissociate themselves from the church leaders.

In each of these parables, it is notable that Jesus' questions do not arise in response to challenges from his enemies. The initiative lies with Jesus, and he puts his charge directly to his adversaries!

83

32. Is It Lawful?

Paying Taxes to the Emperor, Mk. 12:13-17, (Mt. 22:15-22, Lk. 20:20-26)

Prior to this incident, Jesus' parable of the vineyard had made clear to the Jewish leaders the danger in which they stood for being wicked stewards of Israel. In consequence, Mark records that the chief priests, scribes, and elders now sent some Pharisees and Herodians to entrap Jesus by debating with him. Matthew also notes that the Pharisees and Herodians subsequently plotted against Jesus and sent their disciples to entrap him.

Luke says it was the Jewish leaders who 'watched' Jesus and then sent spies to trap him. All three accounts convey the animosity and malicious intent of Jesus' adversaries.

In this narrative, to understand the significance of Jesus' two questions it is first important to recognise the political context in which the exchange took place.

The Herodians were a party of political nationalists. They had supported Herod the Great as the hope of Israel. They were ever ready to compromise with Rome in order to remain in office. Equally, they favoured anyone prepared to denounce the political status quo!

When Herod died in 4 BC, his kingdom was divided into three parts. The southern sector, Judaea, was then ruled for nine years by Archelaus one of Herod's sons. In 6 AD the Pharisees, angered by Archelaus' mismanagement, secured his removal. In his place, they *requested* Roman rule and a Roman procurator was subsequently appointed by Caesar.

Judaea considered itself to be a theocratic society. God alone was king. The law was the Law of God as revealed in scripture, and prophets were authorised to confront kings in the name of God's justice. It was acknowledged, however, that legitimate claims could be made by the ruling authorities of the day.

The general principle of paying taxes was accepted albeit grudgingly. The problem lay with the payment of a particular tax known as the Tribute tax. This was paid specifically to the emperor using a Roman silver coin called the denarius. On one side it bore an image symbolising *the power* of Caesar and on the other *the divinity* of Caesar.

As a tax, it was hated by the Jews being a constant reminder of imperial supremacy and the subject status of Israel! The denarius was not useable in the temple at Jerusalem. Otherwise, it was in wide circulation. In general, it expressed the stability of law and order, and the *Pax Romana,* 'peace, justice, and toleration' including the privileges of a permitted religion, was widely appreciated by the people.

After opening the dialogue with false compliments as insincere as they were hypocritical, some Pharisees and Herodians put to Jesus the following question.

"Is it lawful to pay taxes to the emperor, or not? Should we pay them, or not?" But knowing their hypocrisy, he said to them, "Why are you putting me to the test? * Bring me a denarius and let me see it. (They did so.)" *Jesus said to them, "Whose head is this, and whose title?" They answered, "The emperor's." Jesus said to them, "Give to the emperor the things that are the emperor's, and to God the things that are God's." And they were utterly amazed at him.*

Jesus' first question immediately brought to light the hidden intention of his enemies. His opponents were well aware of the people's attitude to the Tribute tax. They also knew of the general expectation that one claiming to be Messiah would oppose Roman oppression. If, therefore, Jesus answered, "It is permitted", the Pharisees and Herodians anticipated he would be discredited with the people.

Alternatively, if Jesus answered, "It is forbidden" he would endanger himself with Rome.** Plainly their question was hostile and barbed both theologically and politically.

Jesus' second question, aimed directly at the Pharisees and Herodians, enabled him to take the initiative. There was only one possible answer. His opponents were forced to acknowledge that the coin belonged to the emperor. Subsequently, Jesus rather leaves open what are 'the things of God' as against 'the things of the state'.

Nevertheless, his point is clear. To return the coin to its owner was simply to give back to him what rightly was his. To pay the Tribute tax was not incompatible with one's duty to God! Rome was not taking anything that rightly belonged to God. Any obligations incurred that were due to Rome were simply within the divine order of things! (The Pharisees, in particular, could hardly object to this for it was they who had requested Roman rule!)

It is interesting that Jesus seems not to have had a coin of his own. Also, that in making his reply he made no reference to scripture. The clear principle of his answer has continued to influence discussion on the church-state interface since that time.

----

*It is widely agreed that this narrative is a good example of a pronouncement story that takes the form of a controversial apophthegm. The central section concerning the denarius (vv. 15b-16) is not really necessary to Jesus' reply.

**In Rabbinical debate it was common to ask whether the Law of God in the Old Testament as interpreted by the scribes was 'lawful'. A clear distinction was usually retained between 'It is permitted' and 'It is forbidden'.

----

33. Is Not This the Reason You Are Wrong?

A Question About Resurrection, Mk. 12:19-27
(Mt. 22:23-33; Lk. 20:27-40)

Following the incident of cleansing the temple, the Synoptics tell us that Jesus was beset with numerous questions intended to discredit him with the people or incriminate him with the civil authorities. Now some Sadducees came to him with a question about the resurrection.

The Sadducees were largely a class of aristocratic nobles, powerful, wealthy, and often corrupt. From their number came many of the merchants of the city, government officials, and the High Priests. For generations, the Sadducees had dominated the Sanhedrin, Judaea's ruling council. Politically they were nationalists.

Philosophically they leaned towards Hellenism. As a priestly class centred on a few families of great antiquity the Sadducees claimed direct descent from Zadok the priest. They were strict conformists and would accept no new innovations in the Temple. They maintained the freedom of the individual to interpret the Torah and were themselves fundamentalists.

They were governed solely by the literal meaning of biblical texts no matter how out of date, and they had little compunction about manipulating the text to suit their own purposes when occasion demanded! They refused to accept the legal rulings of Hasidic scholars and would tolerate no new interpretations of The Law. They objected to any interpretation of scripture by the scribes and Pharisees.

Apart from the Sadducees, and notably in the time between the Testaments, others developed much broader views. In particular, the just fate of martyrs in God's cause emerged from the Maccabean revolt. Also, the rise of Apocalyptic literature initiated several different beliefs about resurrection. At the time of Jesus, therefore, despite a traditional belief in Sheol there were many who believed in some form of resurrection, either of the righteous who continued their fellowship with God or of the righteous and the unrighteous together though these were kept separate by some form of divine justice.

Ultra-conservative in their views the Sadducees denied belief in any form of survival after death. They ignored any hope of 'a life to come' and they held the traditional view that following death, the 'shades of the dead' departed to Sheol where they remained until the last day, the Day of the LORD. Intent upon defending this attitude and revealing belief in the resurrection to be absurd the Sadducees now put to Jesus the following question which was spuriously based on the teaching of Moses (Dt. 25:5–10).*

"Teacher, Moses wrote for us that if a man's brother dies, leaving a wife but no child, the man shall marry the widow and raise up children for his brother. There were seven brothers; the first married and, when he died, left no children; and the second married her and died, leaving no children; and the third likewise; none of the seven left children. Last of all, the woman herself died. In the resurrection, whose wife will she be? For the seven had married her."

Plainly the Sadducees' question centres on 'marriage' rather than 'preserving the family name'. Also, implicit in their question is their perception of resurrection as a restoration of normal human relationships in heaven. Jesus immediately corrects this misunderstanding and charges them with ignorance both of the scriptures and of the power of God.

"Is not this the reason you are wrong, that you know neither the scriptures nor the power of God? For when they rise from the dead, they neither marry nor are given in marriage, but are like the angels in heaven. And as for the dead being raised, have you not read in the book of Moses, in the story about the bush, how God said to him, 'I am the God of Abraham, the God of Isaac, and the God of Jacob?' He is God not of the dead, but of the living; you are quite wrong."

Jesus' two rhetorical questions might equally well have been statements. However, he uses his first question to instruct the Sadducees that God has the power both to raise from the dead and to turn earthly existence into heavenly existence. Those who are resurrected are thereby transformed into the likeness of angels for whom marriage is no part of the heavenly order!

With his second question, Jesus refers his listeners to the words of Moses in a different passage of scripture, the episode of 'the flaming bush' (Ex. 3:6). He then extends the meaning of this text to include all who die in God's cause. His argument appears to be that, as Moses declared God to be God only of the living (and this includes the Patriarchs), all who die in God's cause will enjoy continuing fellowship with God after death.

With both questions, Jesus has no hesitation in telling the Sadducees that in denying resurrection they were *quite wrong*, an unusually strong emphasis in the gospels. Indirectly, his questions also emphasise Jesus' own belief in human resurrection other than on the last day!

----

*This text refers to the supposed duty of a Brother in Law to perpetuate the family name and inheritance (Cf. also Gen. 38:8).

34. So How Can He Be His Son?
Concerning David's Son, Mk. 12:35–37
(Mt. 22:41–46, Lk. 20:41–44)

Following Jesus' dispute with the Sadducees about resurrection he was teaching generally in the temple. Scribes and Pharisees were said to be present, and it seems that arising from their discussion mention was made of the common belief that a future Messiah would be a descendant of the House of David. Matthew is quite clear. It was Jesus who asked the Pharisees, "What do you think of the Messiah? Whose son is he?" to which they replied, "The son of David."

Thus, it arose that:

While Jesus was teaching in the temple, he said, "How can the scribes say that the Messiah is the son of David? David himself, by the Holy Spirit, declared,
'The Lord said to my Lord,
Sit at my right hand,
until I put your enemies under your feet'.
David himself calls him Lord; so how can he be his son?"

The text Jesus cites here is the first verse of Psalm 110, which reads,
The LORD says to my lord,
"Sit at my right hand
until I make your enemies your
footstool."

It is important to note the significance of the spelling in this Psalm. The first *'LORD'* refers to Yahweh, the God of Israel. The second *'lord'* (or *Lord*) is ambiguous. Usually, it is just a title of respect addressed to a person of rank especially a king. In this context, however, *'my lord'* is taken to refer to Messiah as acknowledged by David. The sense of the passage, therefore, is "Yahweh said to Messiah, 'Sit at my right hand until I make your enemies your footstool'."

Now, it is widely accepted that in Jesus' time the people of Israel universally assumed Psalm 110 to have been written by David in honour of Messiah. So, when David writes that Yahweh says to *my* lord (i.e., Messiah) 'Sit at my right hand', an honour is implied which extends far beyond any that might be ascribed to just a Jewish king whose chief aim is to restore Israel to her former glory, even a hereditary 'son of David'. It embodies a unique and special relationship to God, which David himself recognised when inspired by the Holy Spirit.

Thus, whereas Jesus' first question seeks to broaden the narrow view of Messiah, his second question defines his argument. If David himself speaks of Messiah as, *'my lord'*, Messiah cannot be 'a son of David'. Together, the two questions emphasise that the Biblical evidence of Psalm 110 was not to be overlooked by the Rabbis in their contemporary and traditional teaching. It also may have been that 'Messiahship' was much in Jesus' mind at this time and, perhaps, strong self-realisation of his own personal relationship to God.

----

35. Do You See These Great Buildings?

The Destruction of The Temple Foretold, Mk. 13:1-2 (Mt. 24:1-3, Lk. 21:5-7)

Jesus had been teaching in the court of the Temple.

As he came out of the temple, one of his disciples said to him, "Look, Teacher, what large stones and what large buildings!" Then Jesus asked him, "Do you see these great buildings? Not one stone will be left here upon another; all will be thrown down."

We are not told which disciple made the comment. Matthew says it was more than one. Luke says it was certain people. The remark, however, suggests a degree of wonderment and surprise at the size and splendour of this imposing structure.

Herod's Temple, the Third Temple, is reported to have been a magnificent building the construction of which was not complete in Jesus' day. The disciples would have seen it only occasionally as much of their time was spent away from Jerusalem. It is hardly surprising, therefore, that almost involuntarily they expressed some amazement at what they saw.

The thirteenth chapter of Mark's gospel is often described as 'the Little Apocalypse' (cf. vv. 7–8, 14–28, 24–27.) Jesus speaks mysteriously of numerous extraordinary and calamitous events leading to the end of the world and heralding the coming of the Son of Man. He will "gather his elect from the winds, from the ends of the earth to the ends of heaven," and the people are to be ready!

It is in this frame of mind that Jesus responds to his disciples' remark. His question is brief and rhetorical. It is easy to imagine that he hoped his companions would not just *look* at the grandeur of the Temple but *see and understand* that it could not last. 'Great building' though it was it had lost its way and for all its splendour was impermanent in the unveiling of the end.

Amongst commentators, it is a matter of debate whether Jesus' question foreshadowed the destruction of the Temple in AD 70. His prophecy may have indicated a permanent end to the Temple, or perhaps an interim event prior to some form of the rebuilding of a 'heavenly Temple'.

----

36. Why Do You Trouble Her?

A Woman Anoints Jesus, Mk. 14:3-9
(Mt. 26:6-13, Lk. 7:36-50, Jn. 12:1-8)

Although the details vary all four gospels carry a story of a woman who anointed Jesus while he reclined at dinner. Mark, Matthew, (and probably John) are thought to share one common tradition. Luke's version appears to be a different tradition.

From Mark's vivid narrative, we learn it was two days before the Passover. The chief priests and scribes were plotting to arrest Jesus and kill him. Assuredly Jesus knew of their intention and seems to have been anticipating his own death.

While he was at Bethany in the house of Simon the leper, as he sat at the table, a woman came with an alabaster jar of very costly ointment of nard, and she broke open the jar and poured the ointment on his head. But some were there who said to one another in anger, "Why was the ointment wasted in this way? For this ointment could have been sold for more than three hundred denarii, and the money given to the poor." And they scolded her. But Jesus said, "Let her alone; why do you trouble her? She has performed a good service for me... She has done what she could; she has anointed my body beforehand for its burial."

Apparently, it was not unusual for a dinner guest or traveller to be refreshed by anointing them with oil. What excited criticism on this occasion was the extravagance of the ointment. Jesus' companions were largely concerned that the costly ointment could have been put to better use. They were oblivious it seems to Jesus' inner turmoil and the silent disquiet that occupied his mind.

Jesus' question offers a gentle rebuke to the woman's critics. Also, perhaps his interpretation of her action as anointing him for burial is significantly deeper than the woman ever intended. Nevertheless, he commends what she has done. We can only imagine the inner sense of foreboding, loneliness and isolation which prompts Jesus' question.

In Luke's Gospel, although the parallel narrative resembles that in Mark there are significant differences. Jesus was a guest in the home of Simon the Pharisee. At dinner, "a woman in the city" entered and, weeping, "began to bathe his feet with her tears and to dry them with her hair. Then she continued kissing his feet and anointing them with the ointment."

We are not told the reason for this extraordinary behaviour. We are told, however, that the Pharisee was silently critical of Jesus. He reflects that Jesus was no prophet otherwise he would have known the woman was a sinner. Somehow Jesus becomes aware of Simon's silent criticism, speaks to him, and says:

"Simon, I have something to say to you." "Teacher," he replied. "Speak." "A certain creditor had two debtors; one owed five hundred denarii, and the other fifty. When they could not pay, he cancelled the debts for both of them. Now which of them will love him more?" Simon answered, "I suppose the one for whom he cancelled the greater debt." And Jesus said to him, "You have judged rightly." Then turning toward the woman, he said to Simon, "Do you see this woman?"

Jesus' two questions are directed specifically towards Simon but do not appear to have any direct bearing on the unspoken criticism which had occupied the Pharisee's mind. Rather, Jesus' parable seems directed toward a different point for which the best explanation perhaps is that the woman's impulsive actions resulted from her belief that her sins had *already* been forgiven. She was not behaving in this way *in order to* obtain forgiveness.

Indeed, Jesus himself makes the point, "I tell you her sins, which were many, *have been* forgiven; hence she has shown great love" (Mk. 7:47). Jesus' first question, therefore, appears to have the primary intention of teaching Simon that in response to forgiveness of sins, gratitude is proportional to the greatness of forgiveness. The greater the forgiveness the greater the love it engenders, a lesson which Simon clearly grasped!

Jesus' second question is fascinating and leads to a dramatic application of his parable. In asking Simon, whether he '*saw*' this woman far more is implied than whether Simon had simply *looked* at this woman. The challenge is whether Simon *understands* what is happening in front of him. Simon had offered Jesus scant courtesy and had been nothing but inhospitable to his invited dinner guest.

By contrast, this woman had been profuse in expressing love to one whom she hardly knew! Simon's attitude was plainly judgemental towards a woman whom he saw as a sinner and 'unclean'. He had no insight into God's forgiving love for her. Jesus' second question, therefore, is a gentle rebuke. It attempts to teach Simon the difference between loving penitence and unloving righteousness. It is a question that echoes down the ages!

----

37. Simon, Are You Asleep?

Gethsemane, Mk. 14:32–42
(Mt. 26:36–46, Lk. 22:40–46)

Following the Passover meal, Jesus and his disciples went out to the Mount of Olives. When they came to the place called Gethsemane, Jesus told the others to remain there while he drew aside to pray. Taking with him Peter, James and John, it became apparent that Jesus was extremely agitated and distressed. The words of the Greek text indicate bewilderment and distraction, a fearful sense of impending horror from which Jesus could not escape.

He said to them, *"I am deeply grieved, even to death; remain here and keep awake."* Then, drawing away a little further (Luke suggests about "a stone's throw") Jesus threw himself upon the ground and prayed earnestly that God might protect him from all that lay ahead should that be possible. Returning to the three:

He came and found them sleeping; and he said to Peter, "Simon, are you asleep? Could you not keep awake one hour? Keep awake and pray that you may not come into time of trial."

A second time Jesus withdrew to pray but on returning found his three companions sleeping. Mark tells us that they did not know what to say to him. After withdrawing once more to pray:

He came a third time and said to them, "Are you still sleeping and taking your rest? Enough! The hour has come; the Son of Man is betrayed into the hands of sinners. Get up, let us be going."

Jesus' first two questions to Peter are particularly poignant. Peter was the one who had so impetuously claimed that while others might desert Jesus he would not. "Even though I must die with you," Peter had said, "I will not deny you" (v. 31).

Now, when Jesus asks him, "Could you not keep awake one hour?" surely there is an element of gentle reproach in the question. Also, when Jesus returns the third time his question to the three further suggests a degree of disillusionment and disappointment that they seemed not to comprehend his sense of isolation and abandonment.

Interestingly, In Luke's shorter account Jesus' question is simply, *"Why are you sleeping?"* In effect, this asks how it can be that his disciples sleep when they know him to be so troubled? Luke's comment that they were 'sleeping for sorrow' sometimes is interpreted as suggesting their sleep resulting from the nervous exhaustion of grief and anxiety.

In this narrative, it is clear that the immanence of Jesus' messianic suffering bore upon him heavily. His questions reflect not only the need for human fellowship and the understanding of close companions. They also echo his sense of spiritual loneliness when, at Bethany, a woman in the house of Simon anointed him.

----

38. How Can You Come out with Swords?

Jesus is Arrested, Mk. 14:48–52
(Mt. 26:55–56, Lk. 22:52–53, Jn. 18:2–11)

The scene is the Garden of Gethsemane. Probably it is night-time. John mentions that the people came bearing lanterns and torches! Judas has just betrayed Jesus with a kiss. A crowd 'from the chief priests and scribes and elders' then laid hands on Jesus and arrested him. Luke includes 'the officers of the Temple police'.

Then Jesus said to them, "Have you come out with swords and clubs to arrest me as though I were a bandit? Day after day I was with you in the temple teaching, and you did not arrest me."

Plainly, Jesus is contemptuous of the method used to arrest him. He resents the use of force and its implication that he is some form of an irresponsible revolutionary who would resist arrest. He is a teacher, not a bandit! Never has he attempted to hideaway. Never has he hidden his teaching.

Day after day he was in the Temple in full sight of everyone. What reason could they have for not arresting him then? Presumably, it was because they feared his many followers would be outraged. So, now they came at night which simply betrays the weakness of their cause!

It is interesting to note in Jesus' question his sense of defensive pride at being humiliated and treated unworthily by the Sanhedrin.

----

39. My God, My God, Why Have You Forsaken Me?

Jesus Dies on the Cross, Mk. 15:33–34
(Mt. 27:45–54, Lk. 23:44–46)

It was the day of Jesus' crucifixion and Mark tells us:

When it was noon, darkness came over the whole land until three in the afternoon. At 3 o'clock Jesus cried out with a loud voice, "Eloi, Eloi, lema sabachtani?" which means, "My God, my God, why have you forsaken me?"

In Mark, the cry, *'Eloi, Eloi'* is the Aramaic form of the Hebrew, *'Eli, Eli'* reported in Matthew 27:46. Also, in Mark's account, it is not clear whether the darkness to which he refers was actual darkness or a moral metaphor. It might well be eschatological (cf. Amos 8:9). Luke's gospel, by contrast, suggests that Palestine (at least) was in darkness and that physically "the sun's light failed, and the curtain of the Temple was torn in two."

Within this context, Jesus' last cry has been the subject of much debate. Some suggest it cannot be a cry of despair but rather is a cry of vindication, for it is taken from the opening of Psalm 22 which ends in triumph! Others claim this hardly takes the crucifixion seriously and that the cry is one of utter desolation.

It is unimaginable that God ever forsook Jesus. We must trust, therefore, that Jesus' terrible question reveals nothing but a temporary clouding of an unbroken communion between Father and Son. It manifests, nonetheless, the personal agony of the atonement.

Luke's Gospel
40. Why Were You Searching for Me?
The Boy Jesus at Jerusalem, Lk. 2:48–49

Luke's narrative is the only one to describe Jesus as a young boy. He writes that when Jesus was twelve years old, he first went with his parents to Jerusalem for the festival of Passover. Probably the last time Jesus was there was for his presentation (Lk. 2:22–28).

At the age of twelve, however, a Jewish boy became 'a son of the Law' and thereafter followed the rules respecting feasts and festivals. In general, the Law (Ex. 23:14–17, Dt. 16:1–8) required all males to go to the Temple at Jerusalem to celebrate Passover, although following the diaspora this was not always possible for some. There was no legal obligation for women to attend. Nevertheless, Luke tells us that every year at Passover both Joseph and Mary went to Jerusalem.

On this occasion, and unbeknown to them, when the festival ended Jesus stayed behind and his parents did not discover that he was missing until the end of their first day's journey homeward. They then returned to Jerusalem and after searching for three days found the boy in the temple with the teachers, the experts in the Jewish religion, listening to them and asking questions.

When his parents saw him they were astonished; and his mother said to him, "Child, why have you treated us like this? Look, your father and I have been searching for you in great anxiety." He said to them, "Why were you searching for me? Did you not know that I must be in my Father's house?"

Mary's reproachful question expressed the parent's anxiety. By contrast, Jesus' rhetorical counter-questions express only surprise that his parents would not know where to find him. Surely they understood where he must be!

There is a sense of maturity beyond his years in Jesus' questions. They denote not only his unusual relationship with Mary and Joseph but also an extraordinary self-understanding of his relationship to God as his Father.

Presumably, Luke included this narrative to reflect the early glimmerings of a divine call that could not be ignored.

✓

12/11/22.

41. What Credit Is That to You?
Love Your Enemies, Lk. 6:32–34 (Mt. 5:44–48)

There is a part of Jesus' Sermon on the Plain (Lk. 6:17–49) which centres on Christian love (*agape**) as the guiding principle for human conduct. It includes a series of uncompromising requirements regarding entrance to the kingdom of heaven and becoming 'children of God'. "Love your enemies, do good to those who hate you, bless those who curse you, pray for those who abuse you, etc. Do to others as you would have them do to you" (vv. 27–31).

Jesus is teaching those who are prepared to listen, and he continues:

"If you love those who love you, what credit is that to you? For even sinners love those who love them. If you do good to those who do good to you, what credit is that to you? For even sinners do the same. If you lend to those from whom you hope to receive, what credit is that to you? Even sinners lend to sinners, to receive as much again."

Jesus' questions are direct and interrogative. He makes it unhesitatingly clear that it credits us nothing to trade in goodwill. Always expecting a return for a gift or a favour, keeping a balance of 'something for something', is incompatible with divine approval. Our aim must be towards that disinterested self-giving conduct which is the revelation of a true relationship to God.

In Jesus' Sermon on the Mount (Mt. Ch. 5–7), Jesus has been speaking to his disciples about the new age that he has come to bring. He has given them several illustrations of how to interpret true righteousness as against righteousness required by the Law according to the scribes and Pharisees. He tells his disciples:

"You have heard that it was said, 'You shall love your neighbour and hate your enemy.' But I say to you, Love your enemies and pray for those who persecute you, so that you may be children of your Father in heaven;" and later he continues:

"....For if you love those who love you, what reward do you have? Do not even the tax collectors do the same? And if you greet only your brothers and sisters, what more are you doing than others? Do not even the Gentiles do the same? Be perfect, therefore, as your heavenly Father is perfect."

In Matthew's narrative, Jesus' questions are less interrogative than in Luke's account. Nevertheless, the message is similar and in Matthew, Jesus' first two questions parallel his first two questions in Luke. There are to be no narrow limits set on the recipients of love.

There are to be no quibbles about who is a neighbour and who is an enemy, no distinctions between Jews and Gentiles, no false division between family and strangers. However difficult it may prove to be; the aim is to strive to love all people in the way that God loves. In Matthew, there is no parallel to Jesus' third question in Luke.

In this series of questions, we are given an interesting insight into the ethical principles which guide Jesus' conduct towards others. They also express a sense of authority that surpasses the Law.

*Agape, the Greek word for 'love' in the sense of seeking the good of another person with disinterested sincerity. It is a benevolent self-giving act of will that takes as its standard God's loving and merciful approach to all.

----

42. Can a Blind Person Guide a Blind Person?

On Making Judgements, Lk. 6:39–42 (Mt. 7:1–5)

In his Sermon on the Plain, Jesus has just spoken to the many people present (v. 17) about the nature of Christian love (*agape.*) He next warns them against being judgemental, encouraging them instead to look towards forgiveness as the better way. Luke's narrative then continues:

He also told them a parable; "Can a blind person guide a blind person? Will not both fall into the pit? A disciple is not above the teacher, but everyone who is fully qualified will be like the teacher. Why do you see the speck in your neighbour's eye, but do not notice the log in your own eye? Or how can you say to your neighbour, 'Friend, let me take out the speck in your eye,' when you yourself do not see the log in your own eye? You hypocrite, first take the log out of your own eye, and then you will see clearly to take the speck out of your neighbour's eye."

Jesus' opening double question emphasises the importance of disciples first receiving instruction before attempting to guide and teach others. Otherwise, they will behave like someone blind leading someone else who is blind. Both will stumble.

The next two questions then warn against hypocrisy and Jesus' wry comparison between *'the log in your own eye'* and *'the speck in your neighbour's eye'* suggests a gentle sense of humour. His point is, of course, that one's own faults may well be greater than those of one's neighbour. So, before presuming to judge others begin by judging yourself! Ensure that one's own behaviour conforms to acceptable moral standards before charging others with misconduct.

In Matthew's Gospel, the parallel to Jesus' last two questions is set in the context of the Sermon on the Mount. Jesus has just been instructing his disciples, "Beware of practising your piety before others in order to be seen by them" (6:1).

He then introduces several practical illustrations, beginning with the following example.

"Do not judge, so that you may not be judged. For with the judgement you make you will be judged, and the measure you give will be the measure you get. Why do you see the speck in your neighbour's eye, but do not notice the log in your own eye? Or how can you say to your neighbour, 'Let me take the speck out of your eye,' while the log is in your own eye? You hypocrite, first take out the log in your own eye, and then you will see clearly to take the speck out of your neighbour's eye."

Plainly, the questions in Matthew's narrative do not open with a parable as in Luke. Rather, they follow a clear warning to the disciples to avoid the danger of being blind to hypocrisy. In both gospels, however, the thrust of the two questions is the same. Avoid hypocrisy! Do not be too quick to see wrongdoing in others. Examine your own shortcomings first. The misdemeanours of others then may appear to be not so great.

It is interesting to note how Jesus uses these rhetorical questions to illustrate the principles of his ethical teaching.

---

43. Why Do You Call Me Lord?
Building on Good Foundations, Lk. 6:46–49
(Mt. 7:24–27)

At the close of his Sermon on the Plain, Jesus poses a further rhetorical question.

"Why do you call me 'Lord, Lord,' and do not do what I tell you?"

In the days of Jesus, the title 'Lord' was usually one of respect as addressed for example to a Rabbi. Here Jesus is making the point that it is quite unacceptable to call him 'Lord' yet fail to follow his teaching and guidance! Saying one thing and doing another is not the way of true discipleship.

To illustrate his point Jesus introduces the parable of 'the wise and foolish builders'. A wise person builds their house on a solid foundation of rock. The foolish person builds their house on poor foundations, ('sand' in Matthew's narrative.) When the rains fall, the floods come, and the winds blow, the wise person's house will stand but the foolish person's house will fall! In a similar way, to listen and act on Jesus' teaching is to build one's learning on the rock. Merely to call him 'Lord' and pay nothing but lip service to his guidance is to build one's learning on the sand!

Whether Jesus' question denotes an element of frustration or is simply a way of introducing the parable that follows is unclear. Certainly, there is in his question a sense of confidence in his mission and more than just a hint of obligation. It encompasses an imperative that those who truly would follow him must heed what he says!

----

44. What Did You Go out into the Wilderness to Look At?

Jesus' Respect for John, Lk. 7:24-26 (Mt. 11:7-9)

John the Baptist was in prison and sent two of his disciples to ask Jesus, "Are you the one who is to come, or are we to wait for another?" When the messengers arrived, Jesus was with a crowd many of whom he had just miraculously cured of their illnesses. He told the disciples to return to John and report to him what they had seen and heard. He then began to speak about John to the people, most of whom it is thought would probably have been familiar with John's recent activities in the desert offering a baptism of repentance in the river Jordan. Jesus said to the crowd:

"What did you go out into the wilderness to look at? A reed shaken by the wind? What then did you go out to see? Someone dressed in soft robes? Look, those who put on fine clothing and live in luxury are in royal palaces. What then did you go out to see? A prophet? Yes, I tell you, and more than a prophet."

This gradual crescendo of rhetorical questions exemplifies the persuasive and entertaining style Jesus sometimes used to develop his discourse. In his play on words, there is a gradual progression from what is obvious nonsense to a climax that is in every way serious and significant. Of course, no one would think of going out into the desert to admire some everyday occurrence as uninteresting as a reed shaken by the wind! Nor would anyone go out into an inhospitable wilderness expecting to find people dressed in all the finery of the royal court.

That too would be ridiculous! So, just what did people go out to see? They went out to see a fine spiritual leader, a true and great prophet; and they were not disappointed. There they found John, no ordinary prophet but one who exceeded all their expectations.

So, Jesus begins his respectful tribute to John, emphasising the important part he has played in preparing the way for Jesus himself. It offers an interesting example of the powerful use that can be made of the rhetorical question in rabbinical teaching.

----

45. To What Will I Compare the People of This Generation?

Jesus and John, Lk 7:31–35 (Mt. 11:16–19)

Following Jesus' tribute to John the Baptist and a short editorial insert by Luke (vv. 29–30) the narrative continues with Jesus saying:

"To what then will I compare the people of this generation, and what are they like? They are like children sitting in the market place and calling to one another, 'We played the flute for you, and you did not dance; we wailed, and you did not weep.' For John the Baptist has come eating no bread and drinking no wine, and you say, 'He has a demon'; the Son of Man has come eating and drinking, and you say, 'Look a glutton and a drunkard, a friend of tax collectors and sinners!'"

Jesus' use of the interrogative double question as a means of introducing an illustrative parable is characteristically Rabbinical (cf. Lk. 13:18, Mk. 4:30). On this occasion, he uses the parable to point out the perversity with which he and John have been received by their contemporaries. As in the children's game nothing John or Jesus did seemed to prompt an appropriate response from the people. Neither John's ascetic life and his call for repentance, nor Jesus ordinary life with his proclamation of the Good News had moved the people to respond.

Although the parable manifests the kindly interest, Jesus always showed in children the purpose of his question on this occasion is to draw attention to the very negative attitude generally extended to John and himself by those of their generation!

----

46. Will You Be Exalted to Heaven?
Woe to the Faithless Cities, Lk. 10:13–15
(Mt. 11:21–23)

In this chapter, we are told of Jesus giving instructions to seventy other disciples. He is appointing them to go in pairs to towns and places which he intends to visit in future (vv. 1–12). If they are not made welcome, they are to go out into the streets and say, 'Even the dust of your town that clings to our feet, we wipe off in protest against you. Yet know this; the kingdom of God has come near.' "I tell you," said Jesus, "on that day it will be more tolerable for Sodom than for that town" (Gen. 19:24–28). Drawing on past experience he then adds:

"Woe to you, Chorazin! Woe to you, Bethsaida! For if the deeds of power done in you had been done in Tyre and Sidon, they would have repented long ago, sitting in sackcloth and ashes. But at the judgement, it will be more tolerable for Tyre and Sidon than for you. And you, Capernaum,
will you be exalted to heaven?
No, you will be brought down
to Hades."

Chorazin and Bethsaida were insignificant towns in Galilee. Both had previously experienced Jesus' works of healing and exorcism ('deeds of power') as a call to repentance. Their response, however, had amounted to nothing less than a rejection of his ministry there.

Capernaum probably reflects the importance of that place as the centre of Jesus' Galilean activity. Many had come there to witness and benefit from his healing ministry. As Jesus' rhetorical question makes clear he was disappointed in their response also to his mission as a spiritual teacher!

The reference to Tyre and Sidon is to two commercial Phoenician cities often denounced by the prophets as wickedly heathen (Isa. 23:1–12, Jer. 25:15–17, 22, Ezek. 27–28). Jesus' argument is that *even they* would have repented long ago had they had the same opportunity as the Galilean towns to respond to his mission! Jesus' cry of 'Woe' to Chorazin and Bethsaida is particularly fierce criticism of both of them, as indeed is his emphasis that Capernaum also will not escape being humbled.

----

47. What Is Written in the Law?
A Lawyer's Question, Lk. 10:25-28
(Mt. 22:34-40, Mk 12:28-31)

Luke's narrative tells us that Jesus recently had set his face towards Jerusalem. He had appointed and commissioned seventy additional disciples to go ahead of him. He had spoken clearly on the judgement awaiting those towns and cities that rejected him and he had rejoiced prayerfully at the reports of success from the seventy when they returned. The narrative now turns to a new encounter and a controversial question of the day.

Just then a lawyer stood up to test Jesus. "Teacher," he said, "what must I do to inherit eternal life?" He said to him, "What is written in the law? What do you read there?" He answered, "You shall love the Lord your God with all your heart, and with all your soul, and with all your strength, and with all your mind; and your neighbour as yourself." And he said to him, "You have given the right answer; do this, and you will live."

This passage and its parallel in Mark are thought to be variants of the same story. Luke's account is thought to be nearer the original. In both narratives, the discussion appears to have been largely amicable and Jesus obviously approved of the answers he was given.

In all three Gospels, Jesus is addressed respectfully as 'Teacher' and despite Luke's comment that the Lawyer's question was put 'to test Jesus', it was not designed to entrap him or discredit him with the people. Rather, it was to seek his opinion. * What would satisfy God in order that a person might gain eternal life? Was there some good deed a person might do here on earth to secure entrance later to the Kingdom of God?

Jesus answers the lawyer's question with a double interrogative counter-question. First, he asks what guidance the scriptures provide. Secondly, he asks how the lawyer understands and interprets what is written. The lawyer answers with a summary of two commandments. The first is from Deut. 6:5, "You shall love the LORD your God with all your heart, and with all your souls, and with all your might." The second cites part of Lev. 19:18, "but you shall love your neighbour as yourself." Jesus agrees with the lawyer's answer and advises him to make them his way of life!

It was not uncommon for Jesus to use questions to draw attention to what was written in the Law. Also, in all three Gospels it is clear that in response to his questioner Jesus' answer reflects his respect for the Law (variously quoted). In Luke's narrative, however, Jesus' counter-questions also suggest a certain disquiet at what he saw as the lawyer's erroneous view of eternal life. It is not something 'inherited'. It is the gift of God to those who live by his commandments.

In approving the Lawyer's 'summary of the Law', Jesus revealed that he did consider some laws 'weightier' than others, especially those which retained the spirit of the Law.

*In Matthew and Mark, the question put to Jesus is set in a quite different context. Jesus had just silenced the Sadducees regarding their views on resurrection when a Pharisaic lawyer (a scribe in Mk) asked Jesus which commandment in the Law was the greatest and this opened a far wider theological debate than the Lawyer's question in Luke. It was calculated that the Law contained 365 prohibitions and 268 positive commandments, all of which were divinely ordained.

Some Rabbis feared that any summary of these laws would create a distinction between the 'heavier' and 'lighter' laws, stressing some and diminishing others. It was, therefore, a controversial issue amongst Jewish theologians whether the Law could or should ever be summarised. The most famous of the summaries, given to a proselyte by Hillel, stated, "That which you hate be done to yourself, do not to thy fellow; this is the whole Law; the rest is commentary; go and learn it." Jesus' teaching often made clear that he did consider some laws more important than others.

----

48. Which of These Three Was a Neighbour?

The Good Samaritan, Lk. 10:29-37

The parable of The Good Samaritan arises directly out of Jesus' discourse with a lawyer who had asked how he might inherit eternal life (vv. 25–28). Jesus questioned him about the law and the lawyer recognised that it stated one should love one's neighbour as oneself.

But wanting to justify himself he asked Jesus, "And who is my neighbour?"

Jesus replied with the story of a man who fell into the hands of robbers who left him half-dead. A priest and subsequently a Levite both saw the wounded man but passed him by. A Samaritan also saw him and was moved to pity. He bandaged the man's wounds and made the necessary financial arrangements for an inn to take care of him. Jesus then asked the lawyer:

"Which of these three, do you think, was a neighbour to the man who fell into the hands of the robbers?"

In answer to Jesus' question, there is, of course, only one reasonable answer which the lawyer gave, "The one who showed him mercy." Jesus then said, "Go and do likewise."

It is notable that the parable Jesus told, together with his following counter-question made no attempt to define a neighbour in terms of the close proximity of people. Three people had come near to the wounded man but two had chosen to pass him by. Only one of the three, and he not a Jew, had acknowledged a moral claim for help. Only he had gone to the man's aid. Only one had *become* a neighbour by *proving to be* a neighbour! A neighbour was not to be defined simply in terms of physical nearness!

When Jesus said to the lawyer, "Go and do likewise." It did not directly answer the Lawyer's initial question. Instead, Jesus had focussed on behaving in a neighbourly fashion. What he sought to instil into the lawyer's mind was that a neighbour is not to be thought of in terms of legal definitions. Rather, it is to be seen as a relationship founded on human love. It was left to the lawyer to realise that his neighbour was anyone who had a moral claim upon him to help them lovingly especially in their time of need. Such a relationship arose from loving someone as we love ourselves!

----

49. A Snake Instead of a Fish?
On Prayer, Lk. 11:11–13, (Mt. 7:9–11)

Jesus had been praying in a certain place and teaching his disciples the Lord's prayer. Luke's narrative then continues with several sayings on prayer the first of which (vv. 5–8) is an interim parable about someone endeavouring to borrow bread from a friend. The purpose of the parable is a little obscure but seems to stress the importance of persisting with prayer if one hopes for an answer.

The initial instruction to the disciples then continues (vv. 9–10) with bold assurances that God will always answer their prayerful requests. Whether or not there is an appropriate way to petition God is left open. Jesus then raises some surprising rhetorical questions which at first sight border on the nonsensical!

"Is there anyone among you who, if your child asks for a fish, will give a snake instead of a fish? Or if the child asks for an egg, will give a scorpion? If you then, who are evil, know how to give good gifts to your children, how much more will the heavenly Father give the Holy Spirit to those who ask him!"

Plainly, the answer to Jesus' first two questions is, "No! No parent would do something so ridiculous, so harmful!" The point behind these questions, however, lies not in their obvious answers but in the logical extrapolation that follows. This is a typical *a fortiori* argument, arguing from a strong premise to the question.

In effect, if humankind though evil yet knows how to give good gifts to their children, surely God the Father who is far wiser and more generous will know how to give the gift of the Holy Spirit to those who ask. The unspoken answer, obviously, is, "Yes, of course, he will!"

Of interest in Jesus' third question is the implicit belief in the sinful nature of humanity inherited from Adam, (*"you then, who are evil"*). It was a belief widely held at this time.

117

50. You Fools!

Against Pharisees and Lawyers. Lk. 11:37-41 (Mt. 23:1-36)

Following Jesus' discourse on prayer, an incident occurred in which he cast out an unclean spirit from a man who was mute, and the man spoke again. The crowds were amazed and gathered about Jesus demanding signs. So, Jesus began to address them.

While he was speaking, a Pharisee invited him to dine with him; so he went in and took his place at the table. The Pharisee was amazed to see that he did not first wash before dinner. Then the Lord said to him, "Now you Pharisees clean the outside of the cup and of the dish, but inside you are full of greed and wickedness. You fools! Did not the one who made the outside make the inside also? So give for alms those things that are within; and see, everything will be clean to you."

This is a difficult passage to interpret. * The altercation began with the Pharisee's silent criticism of Jesus that he omitted the ritual formalities of cleanliness and did not wash his hands before eating. Immediately, Jesus turns back the criticism though his argument follows a somewhat obscure pattern.

First, he infers that the Pharisees are chiefly concerned with ceremonially cleansing the outside of cups and dishes when what really matters is cleansing the inside. Then, suddenly, Jesus switches his argument to the inner cleanliness of the Pharisees themselves. If not physically dirty, their 'inner man' is morally unclean being 'full of greed and wickedness'. Jesus' thrust is that if they think there is a difference, they should seek more to purify their inner being!

Thirdly, Jesus' rhetorical question characteristically takes the form of an *a fortiori* argument. If God made both the inside and the outside (of human beings), then there is no distinction to be made between them! The Pharisees are foolish if they cannot grasp that. The argument is slightly different in Matthew.

Jesus' subsequent response to his own question, which links almsgiving to the achievement of moral cleanliness, is difficult to understand.

*It is not clear why the Pharisee invited Jesus to dine with him. There is nothing to suggest that the invitation arose from what Jesus had just been saying. Whatever the reason, the occasion resulted in Jesus denouncing the Pharisees in a series of woes (Lk. 11:42–44). Although the argument here is not cast in the form of woe, it corresponds closely to the fifth woe in Mt. 23:25–26. The order of events is different in Matthew.

----

51. Are Not Five Sparrows Sold for Two Farthings?
On Discipleship, Lk. 12:6–7* (Mt. 10:29–30)

Jesus had just attended a meal where he had become at loggerheads with the Pharisees and lawyers and had denounced them with a series of woes. Thereafter, when outside, the Pharisees and scribes had been hostile to Jesus seeking to entrap him by catching him out in something he might say. Luke reports that a crowd had 'gathered by the thousands so that they trampled on one another'.

Jesus began to warn his disciples against the rise of Pharisaic hypocrisy. Its true character, he said, will always be uncovered. He then added that secret conversations between the disciples also will always be brought to light. The connection between Pharisaic hypocrisy and any private conversation of the disciples is obscure.**

Luke's narrative next continues with instructions to the disciples. Jesus tells them that rather than fearing men may seek to kill them they would do well to stand in awe of God who truly has authority over the destiny of their bodies and souls. Again, this advice has no obvious relationship to Pharisaic hypocrisy, nor is any explanation offered regarding the disciples' danger of being killed. Jesus then seeks to bolster the confidence of his disciples, encouraging them to focus on the providential care of God.

"Are not five sparrows sold for two farthings? Yet not one of them is forgotten in God's sight. But even the hairs of your head are all counted. Do not be afraid; you are of more value than many sparrows."

In answering his own rhetorical question, Jesus' two remarks on 'sparrows' are more readily understood if they are put together. Plainly the purpose of both is to reassure the disciples that they are precious in God's sight. Jesus' comment regarding God's concern for even the smallest of details then becomes additional evidence of divine interest in the disciples' wellbeing.

*Luke's narrative containing this section of text is not easily interpreted. The logical progression between verses is often obscure.

**In Matthew 10:27, which is part of the apostolic commission, the sense is clear that what Jesus taught his disciples privately he wished them subsequently to proclaim publicly.

----

52. Who Set Me to Be a Judge over You?
A Warning Against the Love of Material Security, Lk. 12:13-21.

In this narrative, Jesus is still in the company of the large crowd of people described by Luke at the start of chapter twelve. A man in the crowd addresses Jesus as 'Teacher' and asks him to give a judgement on a matter of family inheritance. No details of the case are given but it seems that a family property has been inherited by two brothers one of whom would like to realise his share.

Jesus replied with a rhetorical question.

"Friend, who set me to be a judge or arbitrator over you?" And he said to them, "Take care! Be on your guard against all kinds of greed; for one's life does not consist in the abundance of possessions."

Here Jesus' question makes the situation quite clear. Even though the man had referred to him as 'Teacher', he has no personal authority to give decisions concerning property.

Surprisingly, Jesus next takes the opportunity to warn the crowd against greed although nothing in the brothers' dispute suggests that this was a factor. He then tells them the parable of a rich man whose land produced abundantly. Believing it would enable him to 'relax, eat, drink and be merry' the man thoughtlessly sought to lay up ample goods for many years solely in the form of 'my barns', 'my grain', and 'my goods'.

Within the context of this parable, Jesus raises a second question as being asked by God.

But God said to him, 'You fool! This very night your life is being demanded of you. And the things you have prepared, whose will they be?' So it is with those who store up treasures for themselves but are not rich toward God.

Jesus' two questions are interesting. The first is almost biographical in nature. The second emphasises his teaching that God expects more of people in this life than merely seeking material security.

*According to the tradition of Dt. 2:17 an elder brother would expect to receive twice the share of the younger. We are not told which of the two brothers approached Jesus.

----

53. Consider the Lilies

Trusting in God's Divine Providence
Lk. 12:22-31 (Mt. 6:25-33)

Jesus had just warned a crowd of people against storing up treasures for themselves but not being rich towards God. He now addresses his disciples on a similar theme. As the sequence of thoughts is a little awkward, it helps to regroup the verses.

(22–23) Jesus said to his disciples, "Therefore I tell you, do not worry about your life, what you will eat, or about your body, what you will wear. For life is more than food, and the body more than clothing."

The thrust of this general proposition is that biological life is a gift from God, and he will provide for its care and wellbeing. By contrast, what the disciples do with their biographical life is more important than worrying about food and clothing. So, Jesus continues:

(29–31) And do not keep striving for what you are to eat and what you are to drink, and do not keep worrying. For it is the nations of the world that strive after these things, and your Father knows that you need them. Instead, strive for his kingdom, and these things will be given to you as well.

Again, Jesus states plainly that God is well aware of peoples' needs. The disciples, therefore, should focus primarily on striving for God's kingdom, trusting God to provide for them. In support of this argument, Jesus adds:

(24) Consider the ravens; they neither sow nor reap, they have neither storehouse nor barn, and yet God feeds them. Of how much more value are you than the birds! (27–28) Consider the lilies, how they grow; they neither toil nor spin; yet I tell you, even Solomon in all his glory was not clothed like one of these. But if God so clothes the grass of the field, which is alive today and

tomorrow is thrown into the oven, how much more will he clothe you – you of little faith!

The thought is clear. God provides every living creature with the means to sustain the gift of life. Within this natural scheme of things, God considers the disciples to be particularly worthy of his divine care. Accordingly, they are to have faith in his providence!

Jesus now introduces two questions, which are related only indirectly to his teaching on providence. Rhetorically he asks:

(25.) And can any of you by worrying add a single hour to your span of life?
(26.) If then you are not able to do so small a thing as that, why do you worry about the rest?

Plainly, the expected answer to the first question is, 'No'. The implication is that one's life span is entirely in God's hands. It is impossible to add to it by worrying. The argument of the second question, therefore, seems to be that *because* the disciples are unable to alter their life span, *therefore* ('If then') there is no point in worrying about food and clothing.

Although the logic of these two questions is a little strained, they do not seriously detract from Jesus' overall message. In order to pursue their mission the disciples should put their trust in the providence of God and maintain a sensible balance about the necessities of life, not allowing them to dominate.

----

54. Who Is the Faithful and Prudent Manager?

On Being Watchful and Trustworthy, Lk. 12:35–48 (Mt. 24:43–51)

Jesus had just been teaching the disciples not to be anxious about food and clothes while they were seeking heavenly treasure and the kingdom of God. Two parables then followed.

The first, only in Luke, tells of servants being ready and awake to greet their master when he returns from a wedding banquet. The second points to being alert to the unexpected for it is not known when the Son of Man will appear.

At this point, Peter asks, "Lord, are you telling this parable for us or for everyone?" It is not clear to which parable Peter is referring. It could be either of them.

Jesus now answers with a rhetorical question.

And the Lord said, "Who then is the faithful and prudent manager whom his master will put in charge of his slaves, to give them their allowance of food at the proper time? Blessed is the slave whom his master will find at work when he arrives. Truly I tell you, he will put that one in charge of all his possessions."

Clearly, Jesus' counter-question does not answer Peter's question. Instead, it provides Jesus with a platform to slightly change the subject and move straight away into a third parable (vv. 45–48). This concerns trustworthy and untrustworthy domestic managers (faithful and unfaithful slaves) and the treatment they will receive from their master when he comes at an unexpected hour. Jesus is more concerned with teaching Peter what he needs to know than what he wants to know!

At this period in his ministry, Jesus' questions and parables seem to express a sense of urgency. Perhaps he was increasingly anticipating the coming of the kingdom.

----

55. Do You Think that I Have Come to Bring Peace?

Understanding Jesus' Mission, Lk 12:51–57 (Mt. 10:34–36, 16:2–3)

In this section of Luke's narrative, Jesus turns from teaching about the future to understanding the present. He had just warned his disciples about being prepared for the coming of the Son of Man. Now, Jesus uses three searching and challenging questions to speak to them of his present mission on earth and reading the signs of the times.

Do you think that I have come to bring peace to the earth? No, I tell you, but rather division! From now on, five in one household will be divided, three against two and two against three; they will be divided: father against son and son against father, mother against daughter and daughter against mother, mother-in-law against her daughter-in-law and daughter-in-law against mother-in-law.

In answering his own rhetorical question, Jesus directly challenges the disciples' perception of his mission and addresses how they perceive his purpose here. His purpose, of course, is not to bring tribulation into the world. Indeed, in his Sermon on the Mount Jesus praises those who 'bring peace to the earth'.

Nevertheless, Jesus recognises that however regrettable, such is the way of society that the effect of his teaching will be to cause division! His call to discipleship will separate some who accept his mission from those who oppose it, some who choose to follow him from those who do not. Thus, even within the family, clashes will be an inevitable precursor to salvation. Any traditional hope people may have that the coming of Messiah is about to bring peace and prosperity to Israel is false. Before there can be any peace, the last days will know strife and tribulation.

His second question which addresses the same subject is put directly to the crowds.

*He also said to the crowds, "When you see a cloud rising in the west, you immediately say, 'It is going to rain'; and so it happens. And when you see the south wind blowing, you say, 'There will be scorching heat; and it happens. You hypocrites! You know how to interpret the appearance of earth and sky, but why do you not know how to interpret the present time?" **

Clearly, Jesus is critical of the people because he expects them to be able to interpret recent remarkable events occurring within society as readily as they read the weather signs.

However, it is not clear from the narrative to which signs of social crisis Jesus is referring, although the implication is that the task of reading such signs is well within their intelligence. They know perfectly well how 'to interpret the present time'. Stubbornly pretending not to understand is unacceptable, (*'You hypocrites!'*) Jesus' second question challenges their deliberate dissembling!

His third question pursues the same point but is a little obscure.

"And why do you not judge for yourselves what is right? Thus, when you go with your accuser before a magistrate, on the way make an effort to settle the case, or you may be dragged before the judge and the judge hand you over to the officer, and the officer throws you in prison."

There is no obvious connection here with reading the signs of the times. Jesus simply makes the point that it is more sensible for people to decide personally what is the proper way to make their peace with God rather than await the Day of the LORD.

In this narrative, it is not difficult to imagine that all three questions, each of which Jesus answers himself, suggest a sense of urgency. The end of the age is near. Conflicts herald the Day of the LORD. It is foolish not to recognise that the kingdom is now at hand. It is wise to be prepared for it.

*Commentators point out that in Palestine westerly winds blow in from the Mediterranean, southerly winds from across the desert. Also, in this passage, the Greek word for 'time' means 'significant time', 'the end of time', 'a moment of destiny'.

----

56. Do You Think
They Were Worse Sinners?
On the Need for Repentance, Lk. 13:1–5

Recently, Jesus had been warning the people to read the signs of the day and be prepared to repent. As he continues, chapter thirteen in Luke's Gospel opens with reference to an indefinite time and place.

At that very time, there were some present who told him about the Galileans whose blood Pilate had mingled with their sacrifices. He asked them, "Do you think that because the Galileans suffered in this way they were worse sinners than all other Galileans? No, I tell you; but unless you repent you will all perish as they did. Or those eighteen who were killed when the tower of Siloam fell on them - do you think that they were worse offenders than all others living in Jerusalem? No, I tell you; but unless you repent, you will all perish just as they did."

These two incidents are recorded only in Luke. Little is certain about either of them.

Jesus' first question is thought to refer to an occasion when, by Pilate's orders, Galileans were killed while sacrificing in the temple. Jesus' second question refers to a less notable incident, a natural disaster that occurred during the construction of the water supply to Jerusalem.

Underlying both questions lies the doctrine of divine retribution prevalent at the time. It was a common Jewish belief that there was a mechanical relationship between behaving wickedly and a subsequent divine penalty, the extent of the penalty being proportional to the wickedness of the sin. In answering his own questions, Jesus rejects this concept. He says the suffering which befell the Galileans did not occur because they were more sinful than other Galileans.

Their particular fate was not divine retribution for some exceptional wickedness. Similarly, the builders at Siloam were not killed because they were worse offenders than everyone else living in Jerusalem. All the people are sinners, each in their own way.

Jesus' message is far more universal than mechanically connecting personal sin to subsequent suffering in the life of individuals. Nevertheless, his questions do serve to remind the crowd that sin is not without its consequences. Everyone needs to repent, though it is not said from what. Each person, therefore, must seek to free themselves from their own guilt by repentance. If they do not, then collectively as a people they can expect to suffer calamities like the Galileans and the builders. *

As in several of his recent teachings, Jesus' two questions again carry a sense of urgency regarding immanent judgement and salvation.

*It is thought by some commentators that what Jesus is alluding to here is the destruction of Israel rather than to individual Judgements before God.

----

57. You Hypocrites!
A Crippled Woman Healed, Lk 13:15–16

This short narrative sits rather awkwardly between Jesus' teaching on repentance (13:1–9) and the kingdom (13:18–20).

Luke records that Jesus was teaching in one of the synagogues on the Sabbath when a crippled woman appeared who had been so bent for eighteen years that she could not stand upright. She made no request but seeing her Jesus called her over, spoke to her, laid his hands upon her, and cured her. The leader of the synagogue, 'indignant because Jesus had cured on the Sabbath', at once addressed the crowd repeatedly telling them that there were six other days on which they could come to be healed. The Sabbath was not a day for work!

But the Lord answered him and said, "You hypocrites! Does not each of you on the Sabbath untie his ox or his donkey from the manger, and lead it away to give water? And ought not this woman, a daughter of Abraham whom Satan bound for eighteen long years, be set free from this bondage on the sabbath day?"

In Luke's Gospel, this is the third record in the so-called 'Sabbath battle', and the second of Jesus healing on the Sabbath, (6:1–5, 6–11). The issues included what constituted work, what was permitted on the Sabbath and under what circumstances?

In criticising Jesus indirectly, the leader of the synagogue exemplified the unfavourable aspects of strict pharisaic legalism. Jesus, by contrast, was moved by the spirit of the Law rather than the letter and in his response appealed to a more traditional, reasonable, and sympathetic interpretation of Sabbath observance. His charge of 'hypocrisy' was directed at those who pretended enthusiasm for the Law when their real aim was to find fault with him. His defence was then presented as two rhetorical questions.

The basis of his first question was the accepted concession of watering livestock on the Sabbath because it was necessary. Strict interpretation of the

Law dictated that water may be drawn for an animal but should not be carried back and forth in a bucket!

Underlying his second question was a belief, then widely held, that illness was often attributable to possession by evil spirits or the work of Satan. Jesus' act of healing, therefore, was presented as a triumph over the power of evil and victory over Satan. Equally important it provided an example of his teaching that it was better to do good on the Sabbath than merely to avoid doing harm! Always, the positive principle of 'doing good' was ethically more important than any negative 'omission principle' (cf. Mk. 3:1–5). Thus, being a daughter of Abraham, the infirm woman was of far greater importance than cattle and *ought* to be healed even on the Sabbath!

Jesus' authoritative questions put his opponents to shame and delighted the crowd.

---

58. Is It Lawful to Cure on the Sabbath?
Healing A Man with Dropsy, Lk. 14:1-6

This short narrative records the third time Jesus accepted hospitality from the Pharisees (7:36, 11:37). On the present occasion, his host was a leader of the Pharisees and Jesus was going to the Ruler's house for a meal on the Sabbath. Other guests included lawyers and Pharisees who were watching Jesus closely. Luke's record suggests that they were expecting Jesus to do something unusual, perhaps contrary to the Law, and they were intent on catching him out.

We are told that at some point a man who was suffering from abnormal fluid retention in his tissues (dropsy) appeared in front of Jesus. How he came to be there is not clear. The text indicates that he was not an invited guest (v. 4). Whatever the reason, it is apparent that Jesus had compassion for him and was minded to cure him. Also, it seems Jesus had insight into what his opponents were thinking.

And Jesus asked the lawyers and Pharisees, "Is it lawful to cure people on the Sabbath, or not?"

Of course, the lawyers and Pharisees would know all the legal objections to this question, but they did not reply. Perhaps they were disquieted by the possibility that other guests may offer a sympathetic outcry.

*So Jesus took him and healed him, and sent him away. Then he said to them, "If one of you has a child or an ox that has fallen into a well, will you not immediately pull it out on a Sabbath day?" * And they could not reply to this.*

Jesus had addressed this second question directly to his opponents. Immediately it drew attention to what constitutes 'work' and moved the focus of attention from what the Law *states* to how it might be *interpreted*. It forced his critics to acknowledge, albeit silently, that what they would do to benefit themselves he also could do to benefit others in similar situations.

135

Actually, the example Jesus provided suggested an emergency, although this was not the case for the man with dropsy. He had made no request to be healed and could have been healed on another day. But this was hardly the point. Jesus' healing was purely an act of human charity, and it re-emphasised his repeated teaching that within the *spirit* of the Law it was an inherent and positive right to heal on the Sabbath (6:6–1, 13:15–16).

The lawyers and Pharisees had no counter-argument to this challenging question. Unable to reply they remained silent even if unconvinced.

*Commentaries describe 'a well' as an open cistern cut in the rock. Also, it is said, somewhat bizarrely, that whereas lifting the victim out was considered by legalists to be 'work' and therefore prohibited on the Sabbath, letting food down was permissible!

----

59. Which of You Does Not Estimate the Cost?
Preparation for Discipleship, Lk. 14:28–32

Luke records that at this time large crowds were travelling with Jesus, and he had spoken to them about family relationships which they must renounce if they wish to be his disciple. He then put two questions to them in the form of parables.

"For which of you, intending to build a tower, does not first sit down and estimate the cost, to see whether he has enough to complete it? Otherwise, when he has laid a foundation and is not able to finish, all who see it will begin to ridicule him. Or what king going out to wage war against another king, will not sit down first and consider whether he is able with ten thousand to oppose the one who comes against him with twenty thousand? If he cannot, then, while the other is still far away, he sends a delegation and asks for terms of peace."

Strangely, the two questions Jesus puts do not really relate to the earlier matter of renouncing family relationships. They are more directly concerned with preparing for discipleship and counting the cost before embarking on such a venture. Jesus is warning them against the folly of letting enthusiasm run away with them before considering where that enthusiasm is leading. Perhaps the modern equivalent would be, 'Look before you leap!'

In answering his own questions, Jesus is not saying do not leap, only that before doing so it is sensible to think the action through.

137

60. Which of You Does Not Go After the One That Is Lost?

The Lost Sheep and The Lost Coin, Lk. 15:3–10 (Mt. 18:12–14)

At this point in Luke's narrative, we are told that large crowds were travelling with Jesus towards Jerusalem, and he had been speaking to them about the requirements for discipleship. Now, some tax collectors and sinners within the crowd drew nearer to listen to him.

Also present were some scribes and Pharisees who murmured critically against Jesus because he welcomed and ate with these people. He moved about among them, taught them, and encouraged them to repent. By contrast, the Pharisees, although they did not discourage repentance, preferred to distance themselves from 'sinners' expecting the initiative for repentance to come from them.

Jesus, conscious of his opponents' criticism, seemed not unwilling to prick the bubble of their self-righteousness.

So he told them this parable: "Which one of you, having a hundred sheep and losing one of them, does not leave the ninety-nine in the wilderness and go after the one that is lost until he finds it? When he has found it, he lays it on his shoulder and rejoices. And when he comes home, he calls together his friends and neighbours, saying to them, 'Rejoice with me, for I have found my sheep that was lost.' Just so, I tell you, there will be more joy in heaven over one sinner who repents than over ninety-nine righteous people who need no repentance."

Although the significance of individual repentance was the issue that initially prompted Jesus' parable, his story actually centres on *finding* the sheep that was lost and *rejoicing with friends* after it had been carried back lovingly into the fold. Also, the implication here is that the sheep was lost through 'folly and ignorance'. (In Matthew, the emphasis is more on the sheep 'going astray' through 'error', and it is just the shepherd who rejoices.)

Jesus then continues with a second parable which opens with a similar question.

"Or what woman having ten silver coins, if she loses one of them, does not light a lamp, sweep the house, and search carefully until she finds it? When she has found it, she calls together her friends and neighbours, saying, 'Rejoice with me, for I have found the coin that I had lost.' Just so, I tell you, there is joy in the presence of the angels of God over one sinner who repents."

Again, Jesus' question is rhetorical and answered by himself. This time the parable focusses on the diligent *search* for a lost coin and, when it is found, on this being cause for rejoicing with friends and neighbours!

Although it was the importance of personal repentance that prompted Jesus' parables initially, neither of his questions addresses this subject directly. Certainly, however, they speak tellingly of divine love for every lost soul and that God spares no effort to reclaim them.

139

61. Who Will Entrust to You True Riches?
The Dishonest Manager, Lk. 16:1-13

Jesus' parable of the dishonest manager is widely recognised as difficult to interpret. If it finishes at verse seven, which seems to be the case, then the story is of a financial agent (manager) who is rightly accused of squandering a rich man's property and is dismissed. However, before leaving, the manager is ordered to provide an account of his mismanagement. Realising that following his dismissal he will need to be welcome amongst people he knows he considers his alternatives.

Eventually, he decides to persuade those in debt to his master to make out another bill in their own writing substantially reducing the amount they really owe! It is debatable whether the sum to be subtracted is just the interest on the loan. The parable then ends rather abruptly, and we are told (v. 8) that the manager is commended because he dealt prudently with men of the world similar to himself who are shrewder than 'the children of light'. The text clearly implies that wealth is to be handled shrewdly in the world of finance. It also is reminiscent of the old adage that children of light (sons of the kingdom), are 'too heavenly minded to be of much earthly use'!

The narrative then continues with the application of the parable (v. 9). This appears to stress that in times of crisis it is important to make the best use of whatever material advantages are currently available, even if that involves dishonestly using wealth entrusted to you! It is not clear from the narrative who draws attention to this point. Probably it is the manager's master. Possibly it is Jesus, though it is difficult to imagine he would condone dishonest dealing for whatever reason.

Now, against the background of this troublesome passage Jesus puts two rhetorical questions to a group of listening disciples (vv. 10–12).

"Whoever is faithful in a very little is faithful also in much; and whoever is dishonest in a very little is dishonest also in much. If then you have not been faithful with dishonest wealth, who will entrust to you the true riches? And if you

have not been faithful with what belongs to another, who will give you what is your own?"

It is not easy to see how these questions arise out of the preceding parable. The stress (v. 10) is on fidelity in small matters as the key to acting faithfully in larger matters. Similarly, dishonesty in small matters leads to dishonesty in larger matters. The teaching then continues (vv. 11–12), *'If then'* you have acted unfaithfully with (personal) wealth gained dishonestly or with wealth belonging to another, who will trust you with 'true riches', i.e., the riches of heaven?

Plainly, this emphasis on dealing faithfully in matters of wealth is at odds with the earlier narrative of commending a financial manager who proved himself to be untrustworthy. There the message suggests that one's salvation could depend on using wealth cleverly even if dishonestly. By contrast, Jesus' questions stress the importance of honesty in financial affairs. They are more in keeping with his closing comment (v. 13), "You cannot serve God and wealth."

----

62. Doing What One Is Expected to Do
Dutiful Servants, Lk. 17:7–10

Towards the end of his teaching to an unspecified group of disciples, Jesus mentions four different topics with no obvious connection between them and which appear to be separate units. The first (vv. 1–2) warns against causing disciples to stumble. The second (vv. 3–4) encourages rebuking and forgiving disciples who sin. The third (v. 6), which Luke records as addressed to the Apostles, speaks of seemingly impossible things that real faith can achieve. The fourth (vv. 7–10) is a parable.

"Who among you would say to your slave who has just come in from ploughing or tending sheep in the field, 'Come here at once and take your place at the table'? Would you not rather say to him, 'Prepare supper for me, put on your apron and serve me while I eat and drink; later you may eat and drink'? Do you thank the slave for doing what was commanded? So you also, when you have done all that you were ordered to do say, 'We are worthless slaves; we have done only what we ought to have done!'"

This is not an easy text to understand. It is found only in Luke and from the nature of its contents seems to have been addressed to a mixed group of affluent people. The apostles were no landowners in possession of slaves.

Jesus' questions are all rhetorical. The first two challenge a master's *behaviour* towards his slave (servant), indicating that they do not meet on equal terms. The third question (v. 7–9) raises the *attitude* of a master towards his slave. The slave should not *expect* to be thanked simply for doing what is expected of him.

Jesus then says (v. 10), *"So you also etc.,"* making clear that in his parable he is referring to his listeners as the slaves, not the master. They must accept that they are 'worthless' in the sense that slaves bring no profit or gain to their master. In undertaking their duties and fulfilling their duties satisfactorily, the master receives from them only what is his due. Obedience to the master's commands is not an occasion for reward. It is merely what they ought to do.

By this complex use of questions, Jesus' argument appears to be uncompromising. Within an ordinary household, a slave knows what his master rightly expects of him. Similarly, disciples in the Kingdom should know what is rightly expected of them by God. As his disciples, they have no special claim upon God. He holds absolute authority. Therefore, because of their relationship with him, their satisfactory fulfilment of the duties expected of them is simply what they *should* do.

----

63. Were Not Ten Made Clean?
Jesus Heals Ten Lepers, Lk. 17:11-19

In this story, only in Luke, Jesus is on his final journey to Jerusalem. As he entered a village between Samaria and Galilee ten lepers approached him calling on him to have mercy on them. Jesus said to them, "Go and show yourselves to the priests." As they went, they were made clean. * Then one of them, a Samaritan, when he saw that he was healed returned to Jesus and praising God prostrated himself at Jesus' feet and thanked him. It is assumed the other nine were Jews.

Then Jesus asked, "Were not ten made clean? But the other nine, where are they? Was none of them found to return and give praise to God except this foreigner?" Then he said to him, "Get up and go your way; your faith has made you well."

Ten men with the same disease all being healed at once in response to Jesus' instructions is unique as a miracle story in the synoptic gospels. It is implicit in the narrative that obedience to Jesus' directions made manifest the lepers' faith and was sufficient to make them clean.

The point of the story, however, focusses not on the miracle but on the grateful Samaritan. He was a foreigner who in gratitude felt it incumbent upon him to return to Jesus and thank him. Already healed by his faith he further received Jesus' kindly reassurance that he had truly been 'made well', 'rescued' from his destructive illness.

Jesus' questions seem to express some surprise. Also, perhaps, they express some disappointment that none of his countrymen chose to behave like the Samaritan.

*(To be 'made clean' was to be more than 'healed'. It enabled Jews to return to their community.)

----

64. Will Not God Grant Justice to His Chosen Ones?

The Unrighteous Judge, Lk. 18:1-8

Jesus had just been teaching his disciples about the end of the age and the coming of the Son of Man. Now he continues with "a parable about their need to pray always and not lose heart."

> He said, "In a certain city there was a judge who neither feared God nor had respect for people. In that city there was a widow who kept coming to him and saying, 'Grant me justice against my opponent.' For a while he refused; but later he said to himself, 'Though I have no fear of God and no respect for anyone, yet because this widow keeps bothering me, I will grant her justice, so that she may not wear me out by continually coming'." And the Lord said, "Listen to what the unjust judge says. And will not God grant justice to his chosen ones who cry to him day and night? Will he delay long in helping them? I tell you, he will quickly grant justice to them. And yet, when the Son of Man comes, will he find faith on earth?"

In charging his disciples to listen to the judge even though he is unjust, Jesus interprets the parable using two rhetorical questions which anticipate a positive answer. *"And will not God etc.?"* Yes, he will! *"Will he delay etc.?"* No, he won't! Used in this form the questions provide an argument that is characteristically *a fortiori*. Thus, if a corrupt judge who neither feared God nor respected people can be prevailed upon to grant justice to a bothersome widow merely because she irritated him with her continual pestering and he wished to be rid of her, then how much more will a righteous God heed the unremitting prayers of *'his chosen ones'*? *

Jesus' third question is quite different. It bears no obvious relationship to the preceding parable or the two questions arising from it. It is an entirely open question to which the answer could be 'Yes, he will' or 'No, he won't'. In short, it remains to be seen what the Son of Man will find at the Parousia! Also, it is possible to suspect that in asking this third question Jesus entertained some doubts about the success of his mission.

* 'His chosen ones' is an unusual expression which can be broadly interpreted as 'disciples'. Initially, it referred to the Jewish people, later to Christians as 'God's elect' and inheritors of the Kingdom. Also, it was a Jewish view that God should not be wearied by incessant prayer. Three times a day was a sensible compromise! By contrast, Jesus' interpretation of his parable seems to encourage persistent prayer day and night, which God will not find burdensome.

----

65. Who Is Greater?

The Mysterious Discourse at the Passover Meal, Lk. 22:24-30 (Mt. 20:20-28, Mk. 10:35-45)

Luke's setting for this short narrative is the Last Supper in the upper room. Jesus had taken his place at the table. The bread and wine had been consumed and Jesus had spoken of his impending betrayal. The disciples questioned amongst themselves which one of them it could be who would do this.

Luke next records that a dispute *also* arose amongst the disciples concerning which one of them was to be regarded as the greatest. * It is an awkward transition without an obvious connection to what precedes or follows it. Unlike John's Gospel (Jn. 13:2ff), Luke makes no reference to Jesus washing the feet of his disciples and, indeed, it is difficult to imagine that their dispute could have arisen *after* such an event.

Presumably, therefore, it occurred early in the proceedings. Possibly the disciples had been arguing about which of them ought to be sufficiently highly regarded to sit nearest to Jesus at the Paschal meal! Jesus' questions then arose to serve as both a mild rebuke and a lesson in humility and service.

But he said to them, "The kings of the Gentiles lord it over them; and those in authority over them are called benefactors. But not so with you; rather the greatest among you must become like the youngest, and the leader like one who serves. For who is greater, the one who is at the table or the one who serves? Is it not the one at the table? But I am among you as one who serves."

Jesus presages his questions by reminding the disciples that in the Gentile world kings may rule absolutely and even oppressively over their subjects. This is not how the apostles are to understand 'greatness'. Rather, if they would gain a reputation for greatness let them first behave like the most junior in their group. If they would become a respected leader, let them first prove themselves to be like one who serves.

148

Commentators point out here that the Greek word translated as 'serves' is to be clearly distinguished from the work undertaken by slaves at the command of their master. Jesus is speaking of a personal service given willingly to supply the needs of others. He then exemplifies his teaching with two interrogative questions related to the familiar domestic scene of waiting at the table.

There are those upon whom one waits and those who unselfishly wait upon them. His questions simply emphasise that any disciple who would be a leader must first be like one who serves willingly, as indeed he always has served their needs.

*A similar discourse appears in Matthew and Mark long before the Last Supper. There, it centres on 'greatness' as a position of honour, authority, and special dignity when Jesus comes to his kingdom in glory.

----

66. The Kiss

On the Mount of Olives, Lk. 22:47–48
(Mt. 26:48–50, Mk. 14:44–46)

The scene is the mount of olives. Jesus was in distress. He had come to the Garden of Gethsemane with some disciples and had asked them to remain awake and pray while he withdrew a short distance, also to pray. When he returned, he found the disciples sleeping, Luke says, "because of grief." Jesus then asked them why they were sleeping and warned them against falling into temptation (cf. Mk. 14:32–42).

While he was still speaking, suddenly a crowd came, and the one called Judas, one of the twelve, was leading them. He approached Jesus to kiss him; but Jesus said to him, "Judas, is it with a kiss that you are betraying the Son of Man?"

Jesus' question is recorded only in Luke. Here it appears to prevent Judas from actually kissing Jesus. "*He approached – but Jesus said to him.*" Certainly, Jesus' question is forceful, and his use of the messianic title Son of Man strongly emphasised to Judas the enormity of his treachery. Surely, we can see also in Jesus' question a reflection of our Lord's deep sorrow. One whom he had believed to be a friend now betrays him to the enemy with an act of false affection.

Jesus' rebuke is worded quite differently in Matthew. After being kissed by Judas, Jesus simply says to him, "Friend, do what you have to do." In Mark, no rebuke is recorded, only the betrayer's kiss.

----

67. What Will Happen When the Wood Is Dry?
The Way to The Cross, Lk. 23:28–31

Jesus was being led to the place of crucifixion. Behind him, Simon of Cyrene had been made to carry the cross. Many people followed Jesus, including women 'beating their breasts and wailing for him'.

But Jesus turned to them and said, "Daughters of Jerusalem, do not weep for me, but weep for yourselves and your children. For the days are surely coming when they will say, 'Blessed are the barren, and the wombs that never bore, and the breasts that never nursed.' Then they will begin to say to the mountains, 'Fall on us; and to the hills, 'Cover us.' For if they do this when the wood is green, what will happen when it is dry?"

Luke's narrative does not appear in the other Gospels. It is a strangely obscure text forewarning the inhabitants of Jerusalem of the different ways in which afflictions will fall upon them.

First, Jesus proclaims not only that women should weep for themselves and their children rather than for him but also that barren women, normally pitied in the Jewish patriarchal society, will be spared the pain of seeing their children perish. Secondly, he pronounces that there will be Jews who think death preferable to the catastrophic times which lie ahead though these are not specified. Here, Jesus is quoting a passage from Hosea 10:8 about the hills surrounding Jerusalem. Thirdly, Jesus presents a rhetorical question in the form of a proverb. This is difficult to understand and despite the use of *'For'*, it does not really connect with his preceding pronouncements.

In its present context, the proverb suggests an *a fortiori* argument. If, when times are favourable, people can cause so much suffering to one who has come to save them, then in the future when times are unfavourable how much more will be the suffering of those guilty of Messiah's crucifixion? It is a question full of foreboding which seems to presage the Last Judgement.

----

68. What Are You Discussing with Each Other?
On the Road to Emmaus, Lk. 24:13–19, 25–27

Following Jesus' resurrection this narrative, only in Luke, records that on the same day that Peter ran to see the empty tomb, Cleopas and another follower of Jesus were on the road to Emmaus talking together about all the recent dramatic events. We are told they were joined by Jesus but were kept from recognising him and did not perceive who he was.

And he said to them, "What are you discussing with each other while you walk along?" They stood still looking sad. Then one of them, whose name was Cleopas, answered him, "Are you the only stranger in Jerusalem who does not know the things that have taken place there in these days?" He asked them, "What things?"

In the circumstances, Jesus' two questions suggest a surprising limitation of knowledge. In the context of Luke's narrative, however, they serve to open a significant conversation enabling the two travellers to summarise the crucifixion event and all that occurred subsequently.

When they finished their account, Jesus gently chided them. Possibly this was because the two looked sad. Or, perhaps, it was because their discourse reflected some confusion between a traditional expectation of Messiah and the unexpected role Jesus had chosen to accept as the 'suffering servant':

Then he said to them, "Oh, how foolish you are, and how slow of heart to believe all that the prophets have declared! Was it not necessary that the Messiah should suffer these things and then enter into his glory?"

Plainly, this third question suggests that the true nature of Messiah necessitated suffering in order to 'enter into his glory'. Jesus then continues and, answering his own question, patiently interprets for them all the Old Testament prophecies as they applied to him.

----

69. Why Are You Frightened?
The Risen Jesus Appears to Disciples,
Lk. 24:36–38, 41–43.

After meeting the risen Lord on the Emmaus Road, Cleopas and his companion returned to Jerusalem where they re-joined a gathering of the eleven and others. The group were discussing Jesus' resurrection and his appearance to Peter, and the two travellers told them of their own experience.

While they were talking about this, Jesus himself stood among them and said to them, "Peace be with you." They were startled and terrified, and thought they were seeing a ghost. He said to them, "Why are you frightened, and why do doubts arise in your hearts?"

Jesus' sudden and unexpected appearance among the group not surprisingly startled everyone. Plainly, they had recognised Jesus but doubted that he was 'real'. They imagined that they had seen a ghost! Jesus' first question, therefore, following his greeting of Peace, seems directed towards calming the frightened gathering. He then encourages them to confirm his bodily reality by looking more closely at his hands and feet, and by touching him. The narrative continues:

While in their joy they were disbelieving and still wondering, he said to them, "Have you anything here to eat?" They gave him a piece of broiled fish, and he took it and ate it in their presence.

This second question is not easy to interpret. Under normal circumstances, it might have been quite normal for Jesus to request ordinary food. It is debatable, however, whether in his resurrected form he required earthly food. Perhaps his question reflects a gentle but explanatory illusion to convince the group of his complete bodily resurrection.

Matthew's Gospel
70. Are Grapes Gathered from Thorns?
A Warning Against False Prophets, Mt. 7:15–20

Towards the close of his Sermon on the Mount Jesus provides several practical examples to illustrate the meaning of his message. He then ends with a series of three warnings often referred to as The Two Ways (the narrow gate and the wide gate), The Two Trees (good trees and bad trees), and The Two Foundations, (the foundations of rock and sand).

Speaking to the second of these warnings Jesus says:

"Beware of false prophets, who come to you in sheep's clothing but inwardly are ravenous wolves. You will know them by their fruits. Are grapes gathered from thorns, or figs from thistles? In the same way, every good tree bears good fruit, but the bad tree bears bad fruit. Every tree that does not bear good fruit is cut down and thrown into the fire. Thus you will know them by their fruits."

The analogy of recognising trees by their fruits was widely recognised in Jewish tradition. Jesus uses it here as the grounding for his rhetorical question. Obviously, the unspoken answer to his question is, 'No!' Grapes are not gathered from thorns or figs from thistles.

In answering his own question, Jesus speaks emphatically against false prophets who will lead people astray. (A similar point is made in Luke 6:43–45). Commentators note that as Matthew's narrative was written towards the end of the first century, probably Jesus' question would carry added significance warning the young church to be prudent in discerning true prophets from deceitful and dangerous enemies.

----

71. Do You Believe that
I Am Able to Do This?
Jesus Heals Two Blind Men, Mt. 9:27–30

Jesus was at Capernaum. He had just visited the house of the leader of the synagogue where he had healed the leader's daughter.

As Jesus went on from there, two blind men followed him, crying loudly, "Have mercy on us Son of David!" When he entered the house, the blind men came to him; and Jesus said to them, "Do you believe that I am able to do this?" They said to him, "Yes, Lord." Then he touched their eyes and said, "According to your faith let it be done to you." And their eyes were opened.

The incident described is so like one recorded later (Mt. 20:29–34) that they seem to be two descriptions of the same event. *

It is presumed that the house Jesus entered was where he lived at Capernaum. Obviously, the two men were persistent in following him. They even entered Jesus' house, continually appealing to him as the merciful Son of David to cure their blindness.

It would be comfortable to imagine that Jesus' question and the reply of the two men resulted in their being miraculously healed by the power of their faith in Jesus. Actually, this is not the case. Simply expressing their belief that Jesus was able to cure them did not thereby impose upon him any obligation to restore their sight. Indeed, had Jesus believed it was God's will that it was in the best interests of these two men not to be cured they would have remained sightless, although this would not have indicated that their faith in Jesus was weak! The two men were cured not because they believed Jesus *could* heal them but because, in effect, Jesus said, "So be it" and *touched their eyes*!

Implicit in Jesus' question is the hidden understanding that however strong and fervent is belief in him and his ability to cure, his healing ministry is always performed in accordance with God's loving and merciful purposes for each individual.

*Commentators point out a further unusual feature of Matthew's gospel in which the writer or editor sometimes uses a 'duplication' to compensate for omitting a reference in Mark. For example, in Mark, there are two records of healing a blind man (8:22–26, 10:46–52). In Matthew, the first healing is omitted but *two* men are healed in 9:27–30, (also in 20:29–34, the parallel to Mk 10:46–57). Similarly, in Mark, there are two records of Jesus exorcising a man possessed by demons (1:23–28, 51–21). Matthew omits the first exorcism, but *two* men are exorcised in 8:28–34 (the parallel to Mk. 5:1–21).

----

72. You Brood of Vipers!

Jesus Disputes with the Pharisees, Mt. 12:34-37

This narrative centres on the source of Jesus' power to exorcise demons. It was a contentious issue and to appreciate the force of Jesus' question it is important to understand how the occasion arose.

The people brought to Jesus a blind mute whose condition was believed to be caused by demonic possession. Jesus cured the man so that he could see and speak again. The crowds were amazed at what they had witnessed. They wondered whether Jesus might be the promised Messiah, to whom they referred as the Son of David. By contrast, the Pharisees murmured amongst themselves that it was only by the power of Beelzebub the ruler of demons that Jesus was able to cast out the demon.

Matthew records that Jesus knew supernaturally what the Pharisees were thinking. Accordingly, he challenged them with three arguments. First, if it was Satan who cast out his own demon then plainly Satan's kingdom was divided against itself and could not stand. If it was Jesus who exorcised the demon by the Spirit of God, then the Spirit was stronger than Satan.

Either way, the power of Satan was broken. Secondly, if they perceived the result of Jesus' exorcism as good let them attribute the power to God's Spirit. If they perceived the result as evil, then attribute it to the power of Satan. Be consistent in their accusations. Thirdly, the Pharisees themselves practised exorcism.

Did they consider themselves to be the agents of Beelzebub? If not, it was sheer hypocrisy on their part to accuse Jesus of using Satanic measures in his healing ministry. To attribute to Beelzebub the virtuous work of God's Spirit was an unforgivable blasphemy! (Cf. Mk. 3:22–27, Lk. 11:14–23).

Moving forwards Jesus then directed his attack specifically at his enemies.

"You brood of vipers! How can you speak good things, when you are evil? For out of the abundance of the heart the mouth speaks. The good person brings good things out of a good treasure, and the evil person brings evil things out of

an evil treasure. I tell you, on the day of judgement you will have to give an account of every careless word you utter; for by your words you will be justified, and by your words you will be condemned."

Jesus' argument is unrelenting. It had become the very nature of his opponents to make malicious judgements and to see only wickedness where there was a virtue. They had lost the ability to speak well of God's Spirit or to see the work of the Spirit as revealed in Jesus. It simply was not acceptable for them to plead weakly that their remarks were only careless and thoughtless talk amongst themselves. Their words revealed what filled their hearts and minds, and by those words, they would be judged!

Jesus' blistering denouncement of the Pharisees is both explicit and authoritative. His question is forceful, *"How can you speak good things, when you are evil?"*

----

73. Have You Understood All this?
Understanding Jesus' teaching, Mt. 13:51

Towards the close of the third section of Matthew's gospel Jesus puts to his disciples a question which though clear and direct yet holds a significance beyond its seeming simplicity.

Matthew records that Jesus had been sitting beside the sea when a large crowd gathered about him. So, he got into a boat and sat just offshore from where he could address the crowd on the beach. He told them four parables concerning the Kingdom of Heaven, the parables of 'the sower', 'the weeds', 'the mustard seed' and 'the yeast' (compare Mk. 4:1–34). Subsequently, when alone with his disciples they asked him to explain the parable of 'the weeds in the field'. After he had done so, he told them three further parables ('the treasure in the field', 'the pearl' and 'the drag-net').

This discourse seems to reflect Jesus' experience of the different abilities of the two groups to understand his parables. The disciples had become familiar with his teaching. They had learned something of the secrets of the Kingdom and anticipated its coming. This was not so for many Jewish people.

They had heard little of the nearness of a Messianic kingdom or of the possibility of resurrection before the Last Day. Thus, although the crowds listened with interest to Jesus' parables, they often failed to hear the message of divine revelation in this particular form of teaching (cf. Mk. 4:11).

After Jesus had addressed his disciples, he asked them:

"Have you understood all this?" they answered, "Yes". And he said to them, "Therefore every scribe who had been trained for the kingdom of heaven is like the master of a household who brings out of his treasure what is new and what is old." When Jesus had finished these parables, he left the place.

Jesus' response to the disciples' reply Jesus' is revealing. It particularly elaborates their duty and responsibility as his trained disciples. They must be like the master of a household. They must be able to bring out whatever is needed,

161

whether it is old or new, to meet every occasion as it arises. They must be always ready to provide old thoughts and new to meet the requirements of those seeking to learn.

Jesus' question, *'Have **you** understood **all** this?'* was not just an enquiry of passing interest. It was a fundamental question upon which depended many of his hopes for the future and the ultimate success of his teaching mission.

----

74. Why Did You Doubt?

Jesus Rebukes Peter's Doubt, Mt. 14:22–33, (Mk. 6:45–52, Jn. 6:15–21)

Matthew reports that following the feeding of the five thousand Jesus immediately urged the disciples to get into their boat and cross to the other side of the Sea of Galilee. Mark says to the fishing village of Bethsaida. John says to Capernaum. Jesus then dismissed the crowd, bid them farewell and withdrew up the mountain by himself to pray. *

That evening when the boat was a good distance from shore, John suggests three to four miles, the disciples found themselves straining at the oars against a strong adverse wind and being battered by waves in rough water. The gospels then record that early in the morning the disciples saw Jesus walking towards them on the sea.

It is useless to try and explain or understand the seeming impossibility of this event. We have to be content simply with the account that the disciples were terrified, believing Jesus to be a ghost, and that subsequently he disclosed himself to calm their fears. In verses limited only to Matthew, the text then continues:

Peter answered him, "Lord, if it is you, command me to come to you on the water." He said, "Come." So Peter got out of the boat, started walking on the water, and came toward Jesus. But when he noticed the strong wind, he became frightened, and beginning to sink, he cried out, "Lord, save me!" Jesus immediately reached out his hand and caught him, saying to him, "You of little faith, why did you doubt?" When they got into the boat, the wind ceased.

Jesus' question to Peter is telling. In part, it is a gentle rebuke, but in part, it might also be an expression of disappointment? After the miraculous cures which the disciples had seen Jesus perform, and especially after his recent miracle of feeding a vast crowd with only a few loaves and fishes, how could Peter still have doubts about the nature of Jesus or his care for all of them?

163

*Matthew omits the short report in John's gospel that Jesus withdrew to the mountain when he realised the crowd intended to take him by force and make him a political Messiah to oppose Rome!

----

75. You Hypocrites!

The Tradition of the Elders, Mt. 15:1–9

Jesus' discussion with the Pharisees on ritual handwashing, ceremonial cleanliness, and the distinction between clean and unclean meats has been considered previously in Mark 17:1–21. In Matthew, the parallel narrative presents the Pharisees question slightly differently. Here, their criticism is confined to breaking 'the tradition of the elders'.

Pharisees and scribes came to Jesus from Jerusalem and said, "Why do your disciples break the tradition of the elders? For they do not wash their hand before they eat?" He answered them, "And why do you break the commandment of God for the sake of your tradition? For God said, 'Honour your father and your mother,' and, 'Whoever speaks evil of father or mother must surely die.' But you say that whoever tells father or mother, 'Whatever support you might have had from me is given to God,' then that person need not honour the father. So, for the sake of your tradition, you make void the word of God. * You hypocrites!"

Matthew's narrative is complex. The thrust of it lies with the Pharisees' question, "Why do your disciples break the tradition of the elders?" (The 'elders' were the exponents of the many general principles that had grown up as an unwritten tradition around the Law. Many Jews regarded the authority of this oral tradition as equal to the Law.**) Jesus' counter-question, "And why do you break the commandment of God for the sake of your tradition?" draws heavily on four passages from scripture (Ex. 20:12, Deut. 5:16, Ex. 21:17, Lev. 20:9).

These emphasise the importance of God's commandment to honour one's father and mother and never to speak ill of them. Continuing, Jesus then charges the Pharisees with hypocrisy, citing still a further passage from scripture to illustrate his charge. "Isaiah prophesied rightly about you when he said: 'This people honour me with their lips, but their hearts are far from me'" (Isa. 29:13, the Septuagint).

Plainly, Jesus' counter-question does not bear directly on the initial question put to him by the Pharisees, which concerned ceremonial hand washing before eating. It does present an interesting example, however, of how Jesus sometimes used a counter-question to deflect unwanted criticism away from his disciples. He would then introduce a passage from scripture and use it to bring criticism to bear upon the Pharisees. Who were they to criticise the disciples on the grounds of 'tradition' when in practice they followed their own tradition in preference to God's commandments? That is hypocrisy!

And so it is. Nevertheless, Jesus' clever use of the counter-question still leaves open the matter of whether the disciples were at fault!

*The circumstance to which Jesus refers concerns the tradition that, if a man vowed (took an 'oath') to dedicate all his property to the Temple this over-ruled any filial duty he had to his parents financially (the Corban controversy). Jesus was at pains to show that this tradition was not part of the Law. For the Pharisees to put their own traditional formula before a divine commandment was not acceptable. They had become so obsessed with the many details of traditional exposition that they had allowed them to outweigh any common sense understanding of the spirit of the Law and even to contravene it.

**Later, the unwritten tradition was codified to become the Mishnah and subsequently the Talmud.

----

76. From Whom Do Kings Take Toll?
Jesus Pays Temple Tax, Mt. 17:24-29

Shortly after Jesus' transfiguration on the mountain he and the disciples were gathering at Galilee.

When they reached Capernaum, the collectors of the temple tax came to Peter and said, "Does your teacher not pay the temple tax?" He said, "Yes, he does." And when he came home, Jesus spoke of it first, asking, "What do you think Simon? From whom do kings of the earth take toll or tribute? From their children or from others?" When Peter said, "From others," Jesus said to him, "Then the children are free. However, so we do not give offence to them, go to the sea and cast a hook; take the first fish that comes up; and when you open its mouth, you will find a coin; take that and give it to them for you and me."

In the Jewish tradition prior to AD 70, every Jewish male from the age of twenty was required to pay an annual half-shekel tax to the temple treasury for temple upkeep (cf. Ex. 30:13–15). Matthew's narrative tells nothing of the circumstances that led to Peter being questioned by the collectors or why he seems to have been singled out as the representative of the disciples.

Possibly it was suspected that Jesus and his disciples were departing from the customary orthodoxy of paying the temple tax. Peter's reply, however, made it unequivocally clear that Jesus did recognise the temple.

Sometime later, when Jesus put his three questions to Peter, they did not refer to the temple tax. Instead, they were directed more towards the people from whom the 'kings of the earth' took money for toll or tribute. So, when Peter answered, 'From others' he answered correctly. * Jesus then reverted to the Temple tax. By analogy, he indicated that as the Son of God in his Father's house he was *freed* from paying the half-shekel. His disciples also, as adopted children of the heavenly king, were exempt!

Quite unexpectedly Matthew then closes the narrative with a remarkable story the necessity for which is not clear. To avoid giving needless offence, and also perhaps for the sake of example, Jesus suggests to Peter a course of action whereby the Father will miraculously provide a 'coin' sufficient for two people to pay the temple tax.** Whether this miracle ever took place remains an open question. Certainly, it expresses a belief in Jesus' power over the forces of Nature!

*Monarchs did not take tribute money from their families. Kings exacted local duties (tolls) from publicans.

The Roman emperors demanded tribute money as a capitation tax (Mt. 22:17–21). The Jewish people hated paying tribute money. They saw it as a sign of subjection (Mk. 12:13–17).

**A 'coin' (Gk *stater*) was worth one shekel.

----

77. Have You Never Read?

Jesus Acknowledges What the People Say of Him, Mt. 21:14–17.

All the gospels record that after Jesus entered Jerusalem to the loud acclamations of large crowds, he entered the temple and drove out the merchants and money changers (Mk. 11:11, 15–19, Lk. 19:45–48, Jn. 2:13–17). Mark and Luke record that the chief priests and scribes were afraid of him and kept looking for ways to kill him. By contrast, the people were spell-bound by his teaching.

Matthew records that:

The blind and the lame came to him in the temple, and he cured them. But when the chief priests and scribes saw the amazing things that he did, and heard the children crying out in the temple, "Hosanna to the Son of David." they became angry and said to him, "Do you hear what those are saying?" Jesus said to them, "Yes; have you never read, 'Out of the mouths of infants and nursing babies you have prepared praise for yourself'?" *

The question put to Jesus by the authorities is central to this issue. They were scandalised by the children's shouting and joyous cries which clearly were Messianic! Similar sayings are recorded in Mt. 21:7 and Lk. 13:35 (cf. Ps. 118:36).

Characteristically, Jesus meets this question with a robust counter-question. It could have been put equally well simply as a challenging statement with the addition of a direct tag-question. *"You have read, 'Out of the mouths of infants and nursing babies you have prepared praise for yourself', haven't you?"* The priests and scribes had no reply.

It is interesting that Jesus' question at this time openly accepts the Messianic acclamations of the crowd reflected in the songs of little ones.

*This text is based on Ps. 8:2 (LXX). Commentators point out that the Hebrew word translated *'praise'* actually means *'strength'* but is less well adapted to this context.

----

78. Which of the Two Did the Will of His Father?

Jesus Warns the Authorities They Will Be Replaced, Mt. 21:28-32

On the day after Jesus had ejected tradesmen and money lenders from the Temple, he returned and was teaching there. The chief priests and elders of the people approached him and asked by what authority he was doing these things. Jesus was not an ordained rabbi. Nevertheless, he challenged their right to question him (Mk. 11:27–33). He then asked their opinion on the following parable.

"What do you think? A man had two sons; he went to the first and said, 'Son, go and work in the vineyard today.' He answered, 'I will not'; but later he changed his mind and went. The father went to the second and said the same; and he answered, 'I go, sir'; but he did not go. Which of the two did the will of his father?" They said, "The first." Jesus said to them, "Truly I tell you, the tax collectors and the prostitutes are going into the kingdom of God ahead of you. For John came to you in the way of righteousness and you did not believe him, but the tax collectors and the prostitutes believed him; and even after you saw it, you did not change your minds and believe him."

Implicit in Matthew's narrative is the principle that God accepts those who rebel but then return. (Cf. also, Jesus' parable of the Prodigal Son, Lk. 15:11–3). One son said, *"No"* to his father, but then changed his mind and did as he was bid. He is presented as the *obedient* son who symbolises many of the sinners amongst whom Jesus worked.

The other son said, *"Yes"* but did not do as he was bid. He is presented as the *disobedient* son who symbolises the Jewish leaders. Jesus makes it quite clear that the Jewish people had accepted God's covenant but the Temple authorities by their pretentious righteousness had proved themselves to be unworthy leaders of the people. Their place in the kingdom of God, therefore, will be taken by those whom they despise!

This narrative, only in Matthew, is the first of three consecutive parables with the same prophetic message. (The parable of the vineyard, 21:33–46. The parable of the wedding banquet, 22:1–4). Divine judgement awaits the Jewish nation. What is interesting about Jesus' first parable, however, is his use of two questions to force from the authorities an admission of their own shortcomings and indirectly assert his own authority.

----

79. You Blind Fools!

Jesus Denounces the Swearing of Oaths, Mt. 23:16–19

In Matthew's Gospel, there is a passage spoken of as 'the seven woes', in which Jesus denounces the hypocrisy of some scribes and Pharisees. In the first three of these 'woes', Jesus is critical of their teaching. In the third 'woe', he accuses them particularly of introducing numerous different formulae for swearing oaths.

"Woe to you, blind guides, who say, 'Whoever swears by the sanctuary is bound by nothing, but whoever swears by the gold of the sanctuary is bound by the oath.' You blind fools! For which is greater, the gold or the sanctuary that has made the gold sacred? And you say, 'Whoever swears by the altar is bound by nothing, but whoever swears by the gift that is on the altar is bound by the oath.' How blind you are! For which is greater, the gift or the altar that makes the gift sacred?"

Much as people today may swear oaths 'on the bible' or 'on my mother's grave' so in Jesus' day did people swear oaths according to different formulae. The Jewish leaders were anxious to discourage people from swearing oaths insincerely. So, they sought to make oaths binding by discounting some formulae and acknowledging others.

Thus, for example, it was decreed that it did not count to swear by the Temple, but it did to swear by the gold within the Temple. Similarly, to swear by the altar amounted to nothing whereas to swear by a gift placed upon the altar was binding!

Jesus' questions come as a scathing indictment of such quibbling and perplexing interpretations of the Law. In his view, the Pharisaic distinctions were fallacious, artificial, and foolish. They deprived the Law of its natural and simple meaning.

Jesus' message is clear. A promise or a pledge should be sufficient in itself. Swearing oaths on the Temple, or whatever, made no significant difference. It was far more honest to let 'Yes' mean yes, and 'No' mean no! These statements alone should carry with them the authority of truthfulness and the assurance of being fulfilled. Temple guides who taught otherwise were not worthy to be religious leaders!

----

80. You Snakes, You Brood of Vipers!
Jesus Charges a Generation with Hypocrisy, Mt. 23:29-33.

In the last of the seven 'Woes' in Matthew's gospel, also in Luke (11:47–48), Jesus further denounces the scribes and Pharisees with hypocrisy, this time in building memorials for the prophets.

"Woe to you, scribes and Pharisees, hypocrites! For you build the tombs of the prophets and decorate the graves of the righteous, and you say, 'If we had lived in the days of our ancestors, we would not have taken part with them in shedding the blood of the prophets.' Thus you testify against yourselves that you are descendants of those who murdered the prophets. Fill up, then, the measure of your ancestors. You snakes, you brood of vipers! How can you escape being sentenced to hell?" *

Jesus' argument is not altogether clear. It is based on a Jewish tradition of martyred prophets. However, only one such occasion is recorded in the Old Testament (2 Chronicles 24:20–22).

The charge brought by Jesus seems to be that in self-righteously building and adorning sepulchres to the memory of murdered prophets, the scribes and Pharisees clearly profess to honour them. Their actions bespeak hypocrisy, for on their own admission they claim to be descendants of those who slew the prophets. Thus, while they protest that had they lived in the days of their forebears they would have acted more wisely, Jesus insists that as descendants they have inherited the same spiritual evil. Their attitudes have not changed.

Inwardly, they secretly consent to the deeds of their fathers. Outwardly they behave in ways that mislead people into perceiving them as righteous (Lk. 11:47–48, Mt. 23:25–26). *"Fill up, then, the measure of your ancestors"*, says Jesus, foreseeing perhaps how soon these hypocrites would cry, "Crucify him!"

In this passage, it is not clear whether Jesus' closing charge and question refer to what he has just said or to a dire warning in the verses that follow. There,

Jesus prophecies that the Jewish authorities will suffer for shedding the righteous blood of Christian missionaries (vv. 34–36). In either case, it is a virulent denouncement of the current generation.

*A similar expression and question are used by John the Baptist at the baptism of Jesus. *"You brood of vipers! Who warned you to flee from the wrath to come?"* (Cf. Mt. 3:7, and Lk. 3:7).

----

81. But How Then Would the Scriptures Be Fulfilled?
Jesus Arrested, Mt. 26:51–54

The scene is Gethsemane. While his disciples slept, Jesus, in distress, has been praying. Now it was time for them to be leaving but as Jesus was speaking to his companions a large crowd arrived bearing weapons and clubs. They were led by Judas and had come from the chief priests and the elders of the people. Judas betrayed Jesus with a kiss. Jesus was then manhandled and arrested.

Suddenly, one of those with Jesus put his hand on his sword, drew it, and struck the slave of the high priest, cutting off his ear. Then Jesus said to him, "Put your sword back into its place; for all who take the sword will perish by the sword. Do you think that I cannot appeal to my Father, and he will at once send me more than twelve legions of angels? * But how then would the scriptures be fulfilled, which say it must happen in this way?"

Plainly, in checking the resistance offered to his enemies Jesus accepts the inevitability of the events unfolding before him. Matthew makes no mention of healing the severed ear, (but cf. Lk. 22:50–51).

The first of Jesus' two questions echoes the narrative of his temptation in the wilderness (Mt. 4:5–7). There, the devil set Jesus on the pinnacle of the Temple and challenged him to throw himself off. The purpose was to test God's promise that always he would command his angels to protect Jesus from harm. Jesus' faith in God, however, required no such test of his promises.

Nor would Jesus claim them now. That would be to defeat God's purpose. Also, it would deny Jesus' own prophetic teaching concerning his passion when, as the Son of Man, he would come finally to Jerusalem and be condemned to death by the chief priests and scribes (Mt. 20:17–19).

Jesus second question is a clear recognition of his acceptance of the role of 'the suffering servant'.

*There is no parallel in Mark and Luke. Jesus' reference to 'twelve legions of angels' symbolise the completeness of the heavenly host, equivalent numerically to 72, 000.

John's Gospel
82. What Are You Looking For?
Jesus' First Disciples, Jn. 1:37-39

One day John the Baptist was in Bethany in Judaea when he was approached by priests and Levites from Jerusalem enquiring why he was baptising with water. John explained that it was in preparation for the coming of the expected Messiah. The following day John saw Jesus coming towards him and openly declared his belief that Jesus was the Lamb of God. The day after, when John was standing with two of his disciples, Andrew and another, he again saw Jesus walking by and exclaimed, "Look, here is the Lamb of God."

The two disciples heard him say this, and they followed Jesus. When Jesus turned and saw them following, he said to them, "What are you looking for?" They said to him, "Rabbi" (which translated means Teacher), "where are you staying?" He said to them, "Come and see."

We can only imagine that John's disciples were impressed by the striking remark their teacher had made. John would not have said such a thing lightly. They were moved, therefore, to go after Jesus in the hope of understanding more about him. He had not invited or called them or caught their attention by any unusual action.

Presumably, however, they knew who Jesus was and now it was his personality that drew them to him. Jesus seems to have understood this. So, when he saw them following, he does not ask, "Who are looking for?" but, "What are looking for?"

One can speculate of course that really Jesus did not know what John's disciples were seeking, though this seems unlikely. More probable is that Jesus' question served to focus their thoughts. Their guarded reply, "Where are you staying?" did not answer his question directly but it implied that Jesus was correct in understanding they wanted a conversation with him.

At this time, Jesus was ready to start his mission. It is possible to imagine, therefore, that Jesus, knowing the thoughts of John's disciples, purposely framed his question in such a way that it could be followed by the invitation, *'Come and see'*. Encounter with Jesus has always been the most important method of revealing his nature.

----

83. No Wine!

The Wedding Feast at Cana, Jn. 2:3–4

It was four days since Jesus had been joined by his first disciples in Bethany in Judaea. Now he was in Cana of Galilee some sixty miles north of Bethany where he and several of his disciples were guests at a wedding. His mother was there also. Probably she had come from Nazareth. (Interestingly, Mary is never mentioned by name in John's gospel.)

It seems that as the celebrations continued it came to Mary's attention that the host had run out of wine for his guests. (This misfortune is captured in the old Jewish saying, "Without wine there is no joy!") The narrative then continues:

When the wine gave out, the mother of Jesus said to him, "They have no wine." And Jesus said to her, "Woman, what concern is that to you and to me? My hour is not yet come."

Why Mary approached Jesus over the difficulty with the wine rather than the host is not obvious. It has been suggested that pondering quietly in her heart the miracle of Jesus' birth, his circumcision, his childhood, and the recent testimony of the Baptist, she thought it an appropriate occasion for her son to declare himself and manifest his power. Clearly, Jesus' thought otherwise.

Commentators point out that Jesus' use of the word, 'Woman' at the start of his question is not as terse or severe as it may seem. In the original, it is more a term of courtesy, even endearment, (cf. 19:26–27). However, why Jesus should use 'Woman' rather than 'Mother' has continued to prove puzzling. Some have suggested that being self-assured at having begun his divine work Jesus now felt detached from his family, his friends, and from trivial circumstances. He was motivated now chiefly by the divine power within him, which was directing his future.

The substance of Jesus' question and his following statement are not easy to interpret. It is possible he was aware that the wine had run out and was simply commenting that he did not need reminding of the deficiency. It also is possible that St John wished to impose a double meaning on Jesus' words. The time ('*My hour*') had not yet come for Jesus to declare himself as Messiah.

Within the context of this narrative, the plain sense of Jesus' question and statement seems to be, "Mother, do not concern yourself. Leave it to me. I will intervene at the right time if necessary."

----

84. Are You a Teacher of Israel?
A Pharisee Visits Jesus at Night, Jn. 3:10-12*

In the meeting between Jesus and Nicodemus, the Pharisee is presented as a thoughtful man, a spiritual leader well versed in Jewish national hopes. He was a member of the Jewish court, the Sanhedrin, and it is clear from his approach that he reflects the views of a significant group of Jews. They did not acknowledge Jesus as Messiah but as a teacher from God who could perform wonderful signs! Jesus does not respond directly to this approach.

Rather, in the discourse that follows he emphasises the need to be 'born from above', 'born of water and Spirit', or just 'born of Spirit' in order to enter the kingdom of God. It was not enough simply to wait for the kingdom to arrive. Already there was a new order and a new form of spiritual life relating to the kingdom.

Nicodemus completely misunderstood the meaning of Jesus' teaching and confused his emphasis on 'new birth' with the normal physical process of natural childbirth. So, he asks Jesus, "How can anyone be born after growing old? Can one enter a second time into the mother's womb and be born? … How can these things be?" (The stress here lies on the word, *'can'*. It reflects the total strangeness of 'spiritual rebirth' to a traditional Jew.)

Accepting the surprising naivety of Nicodemus' questions Jesus responds with a counter-question.

"Are you a teacher of Israel, and yet you do not understand these things? Very truly, I tell you, we speak of what we know and testify to what we have seen; yet you do not receive our testimony. If I have told you about earthly things and you do not believe, how can you believe if I tell you about heavenly things?"

Overall, this passage expresses an element of both surprise and frustration. It is not clear in the text to whom Jesus is referring when he says, *'we'*. Presumably, he is speaking collectively of himself and his disciples. They had repeatedly testified to the knowledge of a new spiritual reality and had seen it in action.

Nicodemus of all people, and especially as a teacher of Israel, should have understood the new situation. However, he had been unable to comprehend 'new birth' and now, even after it had been explained to him, he failed to grasp the relationship between such 'earthly things' as practical baptism, and 'heavenly things' such as being re-born into the new order of the kingdom of God. So, as Jesus' second question makes clear, without a complete change in attitude there was little point in trying to explain further. Sadly, Nicodemus simply lacked the necessary spiritual vision to understand.

----

*In this narrative, it is not clear who is reporting what appears to be a secret conversation at night between Jesus and Nicodemus. The whole passage suggests that rather than taking place at the start of Jesus' ministry the meeting occurred towards the end when the Sanhedrin perceived Jesus as a threat and it was dangerous to be associated with him.

----

85. Does This Offend You?

Some Disciples Express Doubts, Jn. 6:60-63*

In this narrative, Jesus' rhetorical question is not easy to interpret. It is useful, therefore, to note the context in which it is asked.

Towards the close of his Galilean ministry, Jesus was teaching a wide circle of his disciples in the synagogue at Capernaum. Recently there had been the occasion of feeding the five thousand. Thereafter, the crowd having misunderstood the significance of Jesus' 'sign' went looking for him in the hope of receiving further food. Jesus then attempted to teach them the difference between ordinary food that perishes and spiritual nourishment which endures forever.

The people were confused. They thought Jesus was referring to the manna that God had sent from heaven to sustain their ancestors in the desert. Jesus responds that while it was true the manna had nourished the physical life of their ancestors and sustained their bodies, eventually, they had died. By contrast when people partake of the bread of heaven they do not die!

His listeners still did not understand and when they asked to receive the bread of which Jesus spoke, he said, *"I am the bread of life. --- I am the living bread that came down from heaven. Whoever eats of this bread will live forever; and the bread that I will give for the life of the world is my flesh."*

John reports that many were troubled by these sayings. Especially, they disliked Jesus' talk of descending divinely from heaven and they murmured against him. The Jews arguing amongst themselves were further troubled by Jesus' remarkable claim, *"and the bread that I will give for the life of the world is my flesh."* They imagined he had spoken literally of giving them his flesh to eat and they failed to understand how this could be. In reply, Jesus sought to explain that he was speaking in spiritual terms, but they remained confused by his teaching.

At the end of the discourse, after Jesus had reiterated what he had said earlier about heavenly bread, John tells us:

When many of his disciples heard it, they said, "This teaching is difficult; who can accept it?" But Jesus, being aware that his disciples were complaining about it, said to them, "Does this offend you? Then what if you were to see the Son of Man ascending to where he was before? It is the spirit that gives life; the flesh is useless."

Jesus' first question acknowledges the disciples' confusion. When he asked, *"Does this offend you?"* it was to ask what they found hard to accept of all that he had said. His teaching was difficult, but it had not been obscure. What they had found incredible was the claim that someone who to them was ordinary flesh and blood could be descended from heaven as 'the bread of life'! They just could not accept that either 'bread' or 'flesh' could transcend their own limitations and give life forever!

Jesus addressed this difficulty indirectly with his second question, although it is not easy to interpret. Clearly, in speaking of ascending to *'where he was before'* Jesus asserts the pre-existence of the Son of Man. Also, however, the phrase *'ascending to'* could be an ambiguous reference to pre-figure his Ascension at the completion of his earthly mission. In other words, if Jesus' incarnation was accepted as the bread of life *descending,* it follows that it would not be surprising to see him *ascending* in his spiritual humanity when his work is done.

As his closing comment emphasises the disciples were to distinguish between 'flesh' in the ordinary human sense, and 'flesh' in the spiritual sense as the necessary counterpart to his origin and essential being.

----

*Analysis of John's Gospel indicates that some sections of the traditional text may have been dislocated. The events of chapter six are thought to precede those of chapter five.

----

86. Do You Also Wish to Go Away?
Some Followers Desert Jesus, Jn. 6:66–70

The context of this narrative is described in the previous section. Jesus' teaching had proved confusing and troublesome to the Jews and his wider circle of pupils and listeners.

Because of this many of his disciples turned back and no longer went about with him. So Jesus asked the twelve, "Do you also wish to go away?" Simon Peter answered him, "Lord, to whom can we go? You have the words of eternal life. We have come to believe and know that you are the Holy One of God." Jesus answered him, "Did I not choose you, the twelve? Yet one of you is a devil." He was speaking of Judas son of Simon Iscariot, for he, though one of the twelve, was going to betray him.

Jesus' first question is filled with disappointment and anxiety. Many of his early adherents had not just turned away they had given up altogether following his mission. Jesus, therefore, now addresses 'the twelve' directly. Was it possible that they *also* might think of leaving and giving up on him?

His question suggests no supernatural knowledge of what their answer would be. In the hands of the evangelist, however, it becomes the vehicle for a touching confession. Peter, as the spokesman for all of them, voices the deep assurance which they had discovered gradually within themselves.

In responding to Peter, Jesus' second question is rhetorical and characteristically rabbinical in form. As a tag-question, it would read, "I chose you, the twelve, didn't I?" Again, perhaps, there is a tinge of disappointment in his question. Despite Peter's confession, Jesus now recognises that the disciples he chose are no longer of one mind. There is one whose faith could no longer be guaranteed.

187

87. Do You Want to Be Made Well?
Healing a Lame Man, Jn. 5:2-6

Jesus was again visiting Jerusalem where there was a festival of the Jews, possibly the Festival of Tabernacles (cf. 2:13).

Now in Jerusalem by the Sheep Gate there is a pool, called in Hebrew Beth-zatha, which has five porticoes. In these lay many individuals - blind, lame, and paralysed. One man was there who had been ill for thirty-eight years. When Jesus saw him lying there and knew that he had been there a long time, he said to him, "Do you want to be made well?" The sick man answered him, "Sir, I have no one to put me into the pool when the water is stirred up; and while I am making my way, someone else steps down ahead of me." Jesus said to him, "Stand up, take your mat and walk." At once the man was made well, and he took up his mat and began to walk.

There are well-recognised difficulties associated with this text. Some manuscripts prefer 'Bethesda' or 'Bethsaida' for the name of the pool rather than the Hebrew (Aramaic) name. Also, (cf. KJV). Some manuscripts include after 'paralysed', *"waiting for the stirring of the water; for an angel of the Lord went down at certain seasons into the pool and stirred up the water."*

Where this is omitted the subsequent reference to, *"when the water is stirred up"* is obscure. There was a belief it seems that this intermittent movement of the water for whatever reason was attributed to divine action and, therefore, had healing properties.

The pool was thought to be fifty to sixty feet long and was surrounded by five covered colonnades, like cloisters. In these covered spaces lay many infirm people who probably had been there a long time. None of them appears to have recognised Jesus. Nor are we told what caused Jesus to single out this particular man. There was nothing supernatural in realising that he had been there a long time.

It would have been common to discover that in his reply to Jesus' question the man was 'playing for sympathy'. Plainly, Jesus thought otherwise. The man really did wish to be made well but did not have the means to reach the pool before the others. So, very quietly Jesus healed him.

This is an unusual record of Jesus' healing. In the later part of the narrative, John records that the day was a Sabbath. This occasion, however, was no part of the 'Sabbath battle'. There is no argument here about 'healing on the Sabbath'. (That came later vv. 15–18).

The man's condition was not urgent. He had made no direct plea to Jesus for help. Jesus made no reference to the man's 'faith' in bringing about his cure. Nor was it an occasion for 'signs' to make manifest Jesus' divine authority to hostile Pharisees or following crowds. This was truly a 'quiet' healing. It was performed spontaneously, and afterwards, Jesus disappeared quickly amongst the people to avoid attention.

The simplicity of Jesus' question is disarming. It assumes nothing. It is open for the man to reply as he chooses. Underlying the question, however, one cannot but imagine Jesus' distress at the prevailing circumstances and his compassion and deep pity for the invalid in such a powerless situation.

----

88. How Can You Believe?
Jesus Charges the Religious Authorities with Unbelief, Jn. 5:42–47

In this passage, John records that the Jewish religious authorities sought to kill Jesus. In their view, he broke the Law by healing on the Sabbath. Also, he called God his own Father.

In the subsequent discourse, Jesus speaks at length of his close filial relationship to God. He emphasises that he can do nothing of himself but only what God grants him the power to do. Also, in support of his claim, he appeals to the testimony of the Baptist, to his own work as God's son in witnessing to the Father, and to the scriptures. Jesus then turns his defence into an attack. He charges his listeners for failing to acknowledge the belief that he was sent from God.

"But I know that you do not have the love of God in you. I have come in my Father's name, and you do not accept me; if another comes in his own name, you will accept him. How can you believe when you accept glory from one another and do not seek the glory that comes from the one who alone is God? Do not think that I will accuse you before the Father; your accuser is Moses, on whom you have set your hope. If you believed Moses, you would believe me, for he wrote about me. But if you do not believe what he wrote, how will you believe what I say?"

The thrust of Jesus' attack is that his opponents do not have within them the love of God! They will accept prophets who come in their own name, but they cannot accept Jesus when he claims to come *'in my Father's name'*; and here it is important to recognise the force of Jesus' argument. It was Jewish belief at the time that there was an intimate, tangible relationship between a person's name and their personhood. Jesus claim, therefore, was remarkable. It claimed not only *to represent* the Father but also *to reveal* his divine character and power.

190

The point at issue is one of different standards, and Jesus' opening question is plain. If the Jewish leaders measure themselves only by human standards, then they prefer the plaudits of their fellow man to any glory God may bestow. So, how then can they claim to believe in God and love him? If, in everyday conversation and conduct, the Jewish authorities do not seek to win God's approval but instead believe there is no higher reward for their action than popular favour from one another, how can anyone credit them with faith in God? The question is sharp and challenging.

Somewhat less challenging is Jesus' second question. Here the force rests on the authority of the Jewish sacred writings. Jesus was well aware that the authority of the Law far outweighed the teaching even of ordinary Rabbis. He appeals, therefore, to the scriptural authority of Moses.

It is not known to which specific biblical passages Jesus is referring, but it is his claim that in writing about the coming Messiah, Moses wrote about Jesus' divine mission. If the Jewish leaders failed to appreciate that, it is hardly to be expected that they will accept the verbal teaching of Jesus. Underlying Jesus' question, of course, lies the serious implication that the authorities reject him at their peril!

----

89. Did Not Moses Give You the Law?
Jesus Teaches with Authority, Jn. 7:19, 21–24

Amongst the dislocated texts in John's Gospel, this one is thought to follow the narrative of the healing of the lame man at the pool of Bethesda and Jesus' subsequent rebuke of the Jewish authorities (see previous sections, Jn. 5:2–6, 42–47). The Jewish leaders had been astonished at the authority with which Jesus interpreted the scriptures.

In their experience, an ability to quote the Law of Moses with such confidence was usually restricted to teachers from rabbinic schools. They had questioned the source of Jesus' learning. He had replied that it did not come from himself. It came from God. Moreover, anyone who truly sought to do the will of God would have recognised that! Jesus then mounts a further attack upon his opponents.

"Did not Moses give you the law? Yet none of you keeps the law. Why are you looking for an opportunity to kill me?"

The crowd answered, "You have a demon! Who is trying to kill you?" Jesus answered them, "I performed one work, and all of you are astonished. Moses gave you circumcision, (it is of course not from Moses, but from the patriarchs), and you circumcise a man on the Sabbath. If a man receives circumcision on the Sabbath in order that the law of Moses may not be broken, are you angry with me because I healed a man's whole body on the Sabbath? Do not judge by appearances, but judge with right judgement."

Jesus' argument is clear, his questions direct. The Law of Moses decreed that circumcision should take place on the eighth day after birth, (Lev. 12:3). If then, it so happened that a boy-child was born on a Sabbath day his circumcision was not withheld on the eighth day, even though that too was a Sabbath. So, if the law of Moses enabled them to make a child whole before God on the Sabbath what cause had the authorities to be angry with Jesus because he did a similar thing for a grown man?

Jesus' questions discomforted the leaders. They had been in haste to accuse him by appealing to the prohibition of healing on the Sabbath. In the event, he had shown that they had lost the inner spirit of the Law.

Following their embarrassment, perhaps it was not surprising that they continued to persecute Jesus.

----

90. Has No One Condemned You?
The Woman Caught in Adultery, Jn. 8:9–11

It is widely acknowledged that this text (7:53–8:11) is not part of John's original Gospel. The incident it describes is thought probably to be authentic but is omitted by the earliest manuscripts and was interpolated at a later time. In its present position, it is an unexpected interruption to the 'great controversy' in chapters 7–8:12ff.

The narrative tells of Jesus teaching in the Temple. The scribes and Pharisees brought in a woman who allegedly had been caught in adultery. They kept insisting that the woman should be stoned to death according to the commands of the Mosaic law (Lev. 20:10, Dt. 22:22f). Also, seeking a way to bring a charge against Jesus, the authorities repeatedly asked him for his opinion. Jesus did not respond. He merely bent down to write (make marks?) on the ground with his finger. Eventually, he stood up and said to them, "Let anyone among you who is without sin be the first to throw a stone at her." He then returned to writing on the ground.

When they heard it, they went away, one by one, beginning with the elders; and Jesus was left alone with the woman standing before him. Jesus straightened up and said to her, "Woman, where are they? Has no one condemned you?" She said, "No one, sir!" And Jesus said, "Neither do I condemn you. Go your way, and from now on do not sin again."

Jesus' opponents had hoped to trap him into making a statement that they could use against him. If he supported the Mosaic judgement, he would be in trouble with the civic authorities. If he discounted the Mosaic law, he would be in disfavour with the people. Either way, it would discredit him regarding any possible Messianic claims!

It is fruitless to imagine what Jesus was writing on the ground. It is sufficient to recognise that he would not be drawn into making a judgement. Implicitly his two questions suggest an interval during which he waited for his words to sink home. They express both the power of his challenge and the frustration of the scribes and Pharisees as they departed.

----

91. Why Do I Speak to You at All?
Jesus In Dispute with The Jews,
Jn. 8:25, 42–43, 45–47

The seventh and eighth chapters of John' Gospel record a long and serious controversy at Jerusalem during which several attempts were made to arrest Jesus. Disputes had arisen about whether he was Messiah. Jesus had claimed to be the light of the world and had presented arguments in defence of his claim. His listeners had denied that his testimony was valid. Jesus had replied that because his opponents were of this world, they judged him by human standards. He was not of this world. He was from above.

They said to him, "Who are you?" Jesus said to them, "Why do I speak to you at all? I have much to say to you and much to condemn; but the one who sent me is true, and I declare to the world what I have heard from him."

Jesus' question clearly denotes his frustration. In this context, his use of 'Why' means, 'For what purpose do I to speak to you at all?' Presumably, he felt it was not worth his bother as his listeners were incapable of understanding! John reports, however, that Jesus did continue teaching and that subsequently many believed him.

Sometime later a number of Jews took exception to a statement Jesus made which they interpreted as being disparaging to them as descendants of Abraham. Jesus immediately pointed out that nevertheless they now looked for an opportunity to kill him. So, while historically it was true that they were descendants of Abraham they were intent upon that which Abraham would not have done. Jesus then said to them:

"Why do you not understand what I say? It is because you cannot accept my word."

This time Jesus' use of *'Why'* means, *'How does it come about that* you do not understand what I say?' And in answering his own question he again charges them with being spiritually and intellectually incapable of accepting his word. They are no longer children of God! If they were, they would instinctively receive the truth of his teaching. They have lost the ability to discern the truth. They conduct themselves more like children of the devil! He then continues:

"But because I tell you the truth, you do not believe me. Which of you convicts me of sin? If I tell the truth, why do you not believe me? Whoever is from God hears the words of God. The reason you do not hear them is that you are not from God."

Once again Jesus' use of *'Why'* means, *'How can it be* that you do not believe me?' And again, he answers his own question repeating that it is because they are not from God. They are spiritually deaf and prefer falsehood to the truth!

With each question, one can imagine that a dramatic pause would follow. Silently, Jesus' hearers would try to collect their thoughts, but they had no answer. They had lost the spirit of the Law and now judged only by human standards, not God's.

----

92. Do You Believe in the Son of Man?
Jesus, the Son of Man, Jn. 9:35–37

This vivid narrative appears only in John.

It was a Sabbath day following the 'great controversy' (Ch. 7–8). As Jesus walked, he saw a man blind from birth. John records no dialogue between them. Jesus, after making mud from spittle and spreading it on the man's eyes directed him to go and wash in the pool at Siloam. The man did so, and his sight was restored. Subsequently, when questioned by his neighbours he could say only that it was a man called Jesus who had cured him. He did not know where Jesus was now.

The man was brought before Pharisees to investigate the matter. They noted that the healer must be a sinner because by working to make mud on the Sabbath he failed to observe the Law. Then they questioned the man and cross-examined his parents to confirm their son's identity and blindness. They re-questioned the man and were baffled when, bravely, he expressed the thought that Jesus must have come from God to be able to perform such wonders. Angrily, the Pharisees drove the man out from their council.

Jesus heard that they had driven him out, and when he found him, he said, "Do you believe in the Son of Man?" He answered, "And who is he, sir? Tell me, so that I may believe in him." Jesus said to him, "You have seen him, and the one speaking with you is he."

Two features arise from Jesus' question. First is the distinction to be made between 'believing *in*' and 'believing *that*'. Thus, when Jesus asked the fellow if he believed *'in* the Son of Man' it was in the sense of 'putting trust' in the Son of Man. The question, of course, is assumptive and leading. Before such trust was possible, it was necessary for the fellow to 'believe *that*' there is a Son of Man. He required information about the Son of Man. He needed to be sure that this information was reliable. Then he needed to accept it. So, the fellow's answer indicated that for him this sequence had not yet occurred. Hence his reply, politely given, "And who is he, sir?"

Secondly, it is notable that Jesus does not here refer to himself as the 'Son of God'. Rather he uses 'Son of Man', an enigmatic title requiring some explanation.

In the Apocalyptic literature of the post-exilic pre-Christian period, notably in the Book of Daniel (7:1–14), we find a prophetic vision of four great world powers represented as beasts. They are superseded by a fifth power appearing from the kingdom of the Ancient of Days, ('an Ancient One', NRSV). He was 'like a son of man' ('like a human being', NRSV) coming 'with the clouds of heaven'. He was presented to the Ancient One and "given dominion and glory and kingship, that all peoples, nations and languages should serve him. His dominion is an everlasting dominion that shall not pass away, and his kingship is one that shall never be destroyed."

This unusual figure, a form of prototype for a man and an angel together, is not Messiah and does not refer to the historical Jesus. Nevertheless, by the time Jesus was teaching on earth Daniel's vision and the title 'Son of Man' had become endowed with Messianic significance. Later, at the time of entry into the New Testament, the title would have been interpreted differently by many people. In the Synoptics, it is unfamiliar and far less well defined. In John's Gospel, it appears much more frequently and is commonly accepted as a Messianic title describing the Son of God.

What Jesus' listeners may have understood by the title is very debatable. It is not surprising that it was unfamiliar to the cured man. Some people would have interpreted it as 'an ordinary man'. Others may have imagined a more glorious figure. Jesus himself never disclosed how he interpreted the title, though in Mk. 8:32 he is explicit about the destiny of the Son of Man.

It seems most likely that, being politically neutral, Jesus used it as a self-designated title partly in protest against the narrow, nationalistic and military concepts of Messiah which prevailed at the time. The association with the vision of Daniel was far less distinctive, far less particular. It expressed a relationship to all humanity not just to 'nation' or 'family'. Also, in Jesus' use, it always included the concept of the 'suffering servant', which never was part of the traditional Jewish understanding of Messiah.

It is clear in the context of this narrative that Son of Man was a safer title for Jesus to use than Son of God. Probably also, in adopting the obliquity and openness of the title Jesus felt it allowed his listeners to interpret its' significance for themselves. Certainly, it enabled him to broaden the concept of salvation to include all humankind.

----

93. Is It Not Written in Your Law?
Jesus Refutes the Charge of Blasphemy, Jn 10:31–38

In the original text of John's gospel, it is probable that this narrative followed verses 1–18 where Jesus speaks often of his close relationship to the Father. When he had done so on a previous occasion (Jn. 8:48–59), the people had sought to stone him. Now: -

The Jews took up stones again to stone him. Jesus replied, "I have shown you many good works from the Father. For which of these are you going to stone me"? The Jews answered, "It is not for a good work that we are going to stone you, but for blasphemy, because you, though only a human being, are making yourself God." Jesus answered, "Is it not written in your law, 'I said you are gods'? If those to whom the word of God came were called 'gods' – and the scripture cannot be annulled – can you say that the one whom the Father has sanctified and sent into the world is blaspheming because I said, 'I am God's Son'? If I am not doing the works of my Father, then do not believe me. But if I do them, even though you do not believe me, believe the works, so that you may know and understand that the Father is in me and I am in the Father."

In this complex passage, Jesus' argument is presented in two parts. In the first part, he puts three questions. The first of these makes clear he understands he has angered the Jews and that the penalty for blasphemy is death by stoning (Lev. 24:16, 1 Kg. 21:10, 13). Jesus also recognised that his repeated claim, 'the Father and I are one' had offended the Jewish concept of God as 'one and indivisible'. Previously, Jesus had repeatedly tried to make plain that his authority and power stemmed not from himself but from the Father, but his words had always been interpreted as denying the unity of God.

Against this background, Jesus' initial question takes his accusers off guard. Implicitly it forces them to acknowledge the goodness of his Father's works.

Explicitly it forces them to frame their charge of blasphemy. Their accusation is clear, "You, though only a human being, are making yourself God."

Jesus' next two questions, put in response to this charge, require explanation. The first (cf. *'your law'*) refers to an occasion in Ps. 82:6 when God takes his place in the heavenly Council that was believed to rule the world. With a Divine Voice, he commissions the surrounding judges for their work, "You are gods, children of the Most High, all of you; nevertheless, you shall die like mortals and fall like any prince."

Here, the psalmist is not denying the unity of God. Indeed, God is forging a vital personal relationship between himself and those he is commissioning to be his delegates and representatives in the world. Even so (the psalmist has, *'nevertheless'*) they will not enjoy immortality. They will die like other mortals. So, the challenge Jesus is driving home is that in the very law to which the Jews are making appeal they must first explain this divine use of the term 'gods'!

Jesus' third question is extended and rhetorical. It stresses that as the law is not to be challenged (*'scripture cannot be annulled'*) the Jews must accept that when the judges were commissioned to their divine work, they did not *call themselves* 'gods' but *were called* 'gods'. This being so the same principle should apply to all who are invested with authority to execute justice in God's name.

It follows, therefore, that Jesus, being consecrated and sent into the world by the Father to do his good work cannot be charged with blasphemy just because he asserts that he is 'God's Son'. (This extrapolation from the lesser (*'gods'*) to the greater (*'God's Son'*) was not unusual in Rabbinic argument as a way of establishing divine precedence.)

In the second part of his argument, Jesus bolsters the thrust of his questions by challenging his accusers to assess his works. They can choose to disbelieve that these are the works of the Father effected through Jesus, as he claims. However, if the works are seen as good and Jesus is seen to have done them, let the Jews accept the quality of the works as a witness to the nature of the person who performed them.

It is interesting to note in the first part of Jesus' argument that his questions again revealed such an unexpected knowledge of Old Testament law that his opponents had no answer to the authority with which he defended himself. They could disagree with his claim, but they could not rightly charge him with blasphemy.

----

94. Are There Not Twelve Hours of Daylight?

Jesus Returns to Judaea, Jn. 11:7-11

Following his conflict in Jerusalem with Jews who had sought to stone him for blasphemy, Jesus withdrew across the Jordan to Perea where the Baptist had worked earlier. Here Jesus received a message from Mary and Martha in Bethany, two miles from Jerusalem. Their brother Lazarus whom Jesus loved was extremely ill. It is not clear what message Jesus sent back to Mary, if any. The Gospel narrative, however, seems keen to emphasise that Jesus had supernatural knowledge of the outcome of his friend's illness and was confident that a delay of two days before setting out was in accordance with God's plan.

Then after this, he said to the disciples, "Let us go to Judaea again." The disciples said to him, "Rabbi, the Jews were just now trying to stone you, and are you going there again?" Jesus answered, "Are there not twelve hours of daylight? Those who walk during the day do not stumble, because they see the light of this world. But those who walk at night stumble, because the light is not in them." After saying this, he told them, "Our friend Lazarus has fallen asleep, but I am going there to wake him."

When the disciples apprehensively questioned Jesus about the wisdom of revisiting Judaea, his counter-question was enigmatic. Possibly it contained a hint of reassurance. We are safe by day; the night is hazardous. Or perhaps it was intended to make a practical point. To do their work, they needed light to be able to see. They could not work in the dark! It is difficult not to feel, however, that through his question Jesus is alluding to something much deeper.

Jesus had spoken previously about being 'the light of the world' (Jn. 8:4). Also, at the pool of Siloam where he had healed a man blind from birth, Jesus had remarked mysteriously that God's work had to be done while it was still light because the night was coming when no work could be done (Jn. 9:4). His question now carries a similar mystical overtone and implicitly raises two points.

First, it suggests that in life we are granted daytime as an appointed measure to complete our work, symbolically twelve hours. Thereafter night-time comes, and it is too late! Perhaps Jesus wished to suggest 'the daytime of his life' had not yet run its course and although his Passion was near, there still was work to be done.

Secondly, perhaps Jesus wished to emphasise to his disciples that while they have the light of the world to guide them, they will not stumble because it will be like daytime. By contrast when night falls, *unless they have light within them,* they will fail!

Undoubtedly Jesus' question is obscure. In context, however, it seems probable that he is speaking mysteriously both of the need for spiritual enlightenment in order to perform God's work, and of the limited measure of time available to complete it.

----

95. Do You Believe This?

Jesus Speaks to Martha of Rising Again,
Jn. 11:23–27

In response to a message from Mary and Martha that their brother Lazarus was extremely ill, Jesus had travelled to Bethany near Jerusalem. When he arrived, he learned that Lazarus had died four days earlier and had been laid in a tomb. Meanwhile, many Jews had gathered to console the sisters.

When Martha heard that Jesus was coming, she went out to welcome him greeting him with words of simple trust in his companionship, even though Lazarus had died.

Jesus said to her, "Your brother will rise again." Martha said to him, "I know that he will rise again in the resurrection on the last day." Jesus said to her, "I am the resurrection and the life. Those who believe in me, even though they die, will live, and everyone who lives and believes in me will never die. Do you believe this?" She said to him, "Yes, Lord, I believe that you are the Messiah, the Son of God, the one coming into the world."

When Jesus asked Martha, *"Do you believe this?"* it is questionable how much she had understood what Jesus had said. His initial words of comfort had spoken somewhat ambiguously of 'rising again' rather than 'resurrection'. Probably Jesus had in mind the imminent miracle he was about to perform. Martha's understanding, however, was conditioned by her traditional Jewish belief in a general 'resurrection on the last day' when the dead 'will rise again'. It was a remote and future event too far away to be of consolation in her present grief.

Jesus' explicit and remarkable reply, which led to his question to Martha, was totally unexpected. His great *'I am'* statement indicated the immediate reality of a *spiritual* resurrection here and now. *"Those who believe in me, even though they die, will live."* So, when Jesus asked Martha, *"Do you believe this?"* he was asking far more than just whether she accepted what he said as true. The heart of his question was whether she also could grasp that in him lay the life and power of resurrection, a gift available immediately to all who could accept him as the Christ.

Whether Martha fully understood Jesus' question is doubtful.

It is interesting that here Jesus' teaching amounts almost to a duality of body and soul. This was quite different to the traditional Jewish understanding of the person as an indivisible unity.

----

96. Where Have You Laid Him?
At the Raising of Lazarus, Jn. 11:33–40

Jesus was attending the gathering of Jews who had come together to console Mary and Martha on the death of their brother Lazarus. Jesus had spoken mysteriously to Martha of believing in him as 'the resurrection and the life'. Now, Mary came to Jesus and kneeling wept at his feet.

When Jesus saw her weeping, and the Jews who came with her also weeping, he was greatly disturbed in spirit and deeply moved. He said, "Where have you laid him?" They said to him, "Lord, come and see." Jesus began to weep. So the Jews said, "See how he loved him!" But some of them said, "Could not he who opened the eyes of the blind man have kept this man from dying?"

Then Jesus, again greatly disturbed, came to the tomb. It was a cave, and a stone was lying against it. Jesus said, "Take away the stone." Martha, the sister of the dead man, said to him, "Lord, already there is a stench because he has been dead four days." Jesus said to her, "Did I not tell you that if you believed, you would see the glory of God?"

Jesus' emotional agitation at the sight of Mary and others weeping expressed much more than his personal grief. It reflected his deep spiritual disturbance at the reality of death. Also, perhaps, he sensed some internal conflict at the simple expression of faith by Mary and Martha that had he been present their brother Lazarus would not have died. Some mourners in the crowd who seemed to have knowledge of the healing at Siloam (Jn. 9:6–7) expressed a similar sympathetic belief.

Jesus' first question is simply an ordinary request for information. It is entirely in keeping with his weeping with his friends when they were sad. There is no attempt here by the Evangelist to avoid a normal human trait.

Jesus' second question is different. It refers (vv. 25–27) to his earlier conversation with Martha and his claim to be 'the resurrection and the life'. Now Jesus gently and implicitly suggests to Martha that because she has believed in him, when Lazarus comes forth, she will witness not just the physical wonder of her brother restored to life but, more importantly, spiritually she will see the inner meaning of the 'sign', the 'glory of God' as the giver of life.

In this narrative, Jesus' two questions express beautifully both his humanity and his divinity.

----

97. Do You Know What I Have Done for You?

Jesus Teaches the Importance of Service, Jn. 13 12

The third part of John's Gospel focusses on Jesus' private teaching for his close friends. In this opening narrative, the last supper is set *before* the festival of the Passover. We are told Jesus knew 'his hour had come to depart from this world and go to the Father'. Also, that Judas was ready to betray him.

During supper much to the amazement of his disciples Jesus got up from the table, took off his outer robe, tied a towel around himself, poured water into a basin and began to wash his disciples' feet. At first, Peter did not understand and tried to refuse an action which he thought too servile for Jesus. When Jesus firmly explained that what he was doing symbolised sharing his life and work, Peter, with characteristic enthusiasm, asked that his hands and his head be washed also! Jesus sought to explain to him that spiritual cleansing meant more than just outward washing, but it is doubtful if he or the others understood.

After he had washed their feet, had put on his robe, and had returned to the table, he said to them, "Do you know what I have done to you?"

As he did so often Jesus then answered his own question. It was important for them to recognise the significance of his action. Even as their acknowledged Lord and Teacher he wanted them to realise that it was still his duty to serve them in love and humility so that they, in turn, may learn to serve one another. Divine power and authority were consistent with ministering humbly to others.

Jesus' question was far from simple. It extended far beyond the example of washing his disciples' feet and introduced an object lesson in humility and the dignity of service.

----

98. Do You Now Believe?

Jesus' Great Discourse with the Disciples, Jn. 16:18–19, 27–32

At the last supper, Jesus identified Judas as his betrayer and Judas left the upper room. What followed is often referred to as Jesus' last discourse with his disciples. *

During this long discourse Jesus referred to himself as 'the true vine' and his Father as 'the vine-grower'. He spoke at length about being in close union with his disciples, of abiding in one another, of bearing much fruit and of loving one another. He warned that the world would hate them because of him.

He encouraged them to testify on his behalf in the power of the Advocate, the Spirit of truth whom the Father will send them. He prophesied forthcoming conflicts which as his disciples they must expect. Also, he explained to them that he had spoken of all these things so that when they occurred his disciples would remember his words.

When Jesus first mentioned *"going to him who sent me"* (Jn. 16:5) the disciples were so startled, so sorrowful and filled with self-concern that they did not think to ask where Jesus was going. So, Jesus continued to emphasise the importance of both him going away and of sending the Advocate to guide and comfort them. Mysteriously, he also spoke of the disciples no longer seeing him and in a short while seeing him again because he was going to the Father. The disciples were puzzled.

They said, "What does he mean by this 'a little while'? We do not know what he is talking about." Jesus knew what they wanted to ask him, so he said to them, "Are you discussing among yourselves what I meant when I said, 'A little while, and you will no longer see me, and again a little while and you will see me'?"

Characteristically, Jesus then answers his own question. He sought to reassure the disciples that through their tribulation of weeping and pain will come the rejoicing of seeing him again. It was almost the close of the discourse and Jesus continues, more explicitly: -

"For the Father himself loves you, because you have loved me and have believed that I came from God. I came from the Father and have come into the world; again, I am leaving the world and am going to the Father."

His disciples said, "Yes, now you are speaking plainly, not in any figure of speech! Now we know that you know all things, and do not need to have anyone question you; by this we believe that you came from God." Jesus answered them, "Do you now believe? The hour is coming, indeed it has come, when you will be scattered, each one to his own home, and you will leave me alone."

Having earlier been perplexed by Jesus' mysterious references to no longer seeing him for a while and then after a while seeing him again, the disciples now welcome Jesus' plain statement and declare their faith. Jesus' response to this confession takes the form of a rhetorical question. He acknowledges their belief but at the same time expresses doubts that they have truly understood the consequences of what they have said. Indeed, his question is almost a statement, "Yes, at the moment you believe, but…!" Jesus could foresee that the disciples would be persecuted for his sake. Their faith would be shaken by events they could not yet imagine, and they would desert him.

The Rabbinical style of Jesus' discourse, which often favours the 'rhetorical question and self-answer' form of teaching, is used here to good effect.

*In John's narrative, there is reason to think that there has been some dislocation of the original text and that the best order is cc. 13:31a, 15, 16, 13:31b–38, 14, 17 and 18. As this seems to favour the questions asked by Jesus it has been followed here.

----

99. Will You Lay Down Your Life for Me?
Jesus Questions Peter's Devotion, Jn. 13:31b–38

At the close of the last discourse, Jesus, despite the disciples' declaration of belief in him, had foreseen that when they were persecuted because of him they would scatter (Jn. 16:31–32). Now he turns to what the Passion will mean to his close friends. He addresses them as 'little children', a term of endearment. Again, he speaks mysteriously of being with them only a little longer so that it will be of no avail to look for him! Meanwhile, they are to love one another as a sign that they are his disciples. As before (Jn, 16:17) the disciples were puzzled by these words and concerned about what would happen to them.

Simon Peter said to him, "Lord, where are you going?" Jesus answered, "Where I am going, you cannot follow me now; but you will follow afterward." Peter said to him, "Lord, why can I not follow you now? I will lay down my life for you." Jesus answered, "Will you lay down your life for me? Very truly, I tell you, before the cock crows, you will have denied me three times."

Plainly, Peter had not understood the magnitude of the danger that surrounded them all. He was naively confident that in the present circumstances he would lay down his life for Jesus. He saw no reason why he could not follow Jesus *now* but would be able to follow him *afterwards*. He had not realised how close was Jesus' Passion.

The narrative implies that Jesus had complete foreknowledge of the events that were about to unfold. His question, which dramatically repeats Peter's own words, is almost a rebuke. In form, it resembles an earlier question to the disciples, *"Do you now believe?"* (Jn. 16:30–31). As before the question is put chiefly as a statement, although this time as a warning also, "Yes, Peter, you say that you will lay down your life for me but...!"

It is implicit in Jesus' question that he foresaw Peter's three-fold denial. It is not clear how much he foresaw of Peter's subsequent devotion or his eventual martyrdom which, according to tradition, occurred c. AD 64.

----

100. If It Were Not So,
Would I Have Told You?
Thomas and Phillip Interrupt, Jn. 14:1–11

Jesus had been speaking of his imminent departure telling the disciples that where he is going, they could not follow. Three times they interrupted him. Peter had been first. He had quite failed to understand the spiritual significance of Jesus' discourse. He questioned the reason he could not follow Jesus and Jesus had rebuked him (Jn. 13:33–38.) Seeking to reassure them Jesus next explained to them the purpose of his departure. This was to prepare a place for them in his Father's house and return to receive them.

"In my Father's house are many dwelling places. If it were not so, would I have told you that I go to prepare a place for you? And if I go to prepare a place for you, I will come again and will take you to myself, so that where I am, there you may be also. And you know the way to the place where I am going."

Commentators point out that this construction of Jesus' question is open to criticism. It is better interpreted as two statements. The first is *"If it were not so, I would have told you."* The second is *"I go to prepare a place for you."* (cf. KJV, NIV).

As it appears in the present text Jesus' question is rhetorical and the expected answer is, 'No!' More important, however, is the sense of trust implied by the question. Jesus had never held anything back from his disciples even when this was worrying or difficult for them to understand. So, he continues first by pointing out the necessity of his departure, (*"And If I go etc."*), and then, secondly, by further alluding mysteriously to them all returning eventually to his Father's house. (This last seems to be an oblique reference to the Parousia.)

In the past, Jesus had often spoken to the disciples of his departure. This time he refers to them, *'knowing the way'*, and the assumption here is that they are familiar with what *'the way'* entails, including his Passion. But this is not so and Thomas, ever the pragmatic disciple, interrupts Jesus for a second time saying quite plainly that as they do not know where Jesus is going how can they know the way? Jesus explains, "I am the way, the truth, and the life," and Thomas is led to understand that one may know the way without always knowing the end of the journey. Jesus then continues, this time to be interrupted again by Phillip.

"If you know me you will know my Father also. From now on you do know him and have seen him." Phillip said to him, "Lord, show us the Father, and we will be satisfied." Jesus said to him, "Have I been with you all this time, Phillip, and you still do not know me? Whoever has seen me has seen the Father. How can you say, 'Show us the Father'? Do you not believe that I am in the Father and the Father is in me?"

Perhaps Phillip's request to be shown the Father so that they may be satisfied seemed aggressive. Certainly, Jesus' questions indicate a sense of profound disappointment. It was not enough that Phillip acknowledged Jesus as the Christ. Phillip obviously did not understand that Jesus' whole life has been a true manifestation of the Father, or that Jesus is in the Father and the Father is in him so that their union is complete. Phillip should have known this. Jesus expected more from him.

These three interruptions had revealed that Peter, Thomas and Phillip still really did not know Jesus despite being with him longer than anyone. Manifestly they had failed to realise the divine unity that existed between Father and Son or the nearness of Jesus' Passion. Had they done so their questions would have been unnecessary. Perhaps it is not surprising, therefore, that Jesus' own questions are filled with sorrowful reproach.

----

101. Whom Are You Looking For?
Jesus Is Arrested, Jn. 18:4–8, 10, 11

At the close of the farewell discourse, and after prayer for himself, his disciples, and the church universal (Ch. 17), Jesus and his disciples left the upper room. They went out into a garden in the Kidron valley, which lies between Jerusalem and the Mount of Olives.

Judas knew of that garden and brought a detachment of soldiers and temple police to arrest Jesus. They were carrying lanterns, torches, and weapons. John's narrative suggests it was night-time and that it might be difficult to identify Jesus in the dark.

Then Jesus, knowing all that was to happen to him, came forward and asked them, "Whom are you looking for?" They answered, "Jesus of Nazareth." Jesus replied, "I am he." Judas, who betrayed him, was standing with them. When Jesus said to them, "I am he," they stepped back and fell to the ground. Again he asked them, "Whom are you looking for?" And they said, "Jesus of Nazareth." Jesus answered, "I told you that I am he. So if you are looking for me, let these men go." --- Then Simon Peter, who had a sword, drew it, struck the high priest's slave, and cut off his right ear. The slave's name was Malchus. Jesus said to Peter, "Put your sword back in its sheath. Am I not to drink the cup that the Father has given me?"

Far from trying to avoid detection as perhaps the officers expected, Jesus faced them. "Knowing all that was to happen to him," he challenged them directly with his question. John makes no mention in his narrative of Judas identifying Jesus with a kiss.

The fact that Jesus made no effort to conceal himself and escape capture not only shielded his disciples, but it also completely overawed his captors. Jesus, therefore, repeated his question and again identified himself. At the same time, he requested that the authorities let his disciples go.

In the scuffle and confusion that followed, Peter strikes out with his sword at their enemies and Jesus admonishes him. Rhetorically, Jesus then puts his question to Peter the substance of which clearly echoes Jesus' agony in the garden as recorded by the Synoptists. *"Am I not to drink the cup that the Father has given me?"*

In John's narrative, Judas does not need to identify Jesus with a kiss. Jesus makes no attempt at concealment. He clearly insists that the authorities name him. The arresting officers do not have to take him by force. It is Jesus who determines the course of events.

All of Jesus' questions seem to reflect that his fate is self-determined.

----

102. Why Do You Strike Me?
Jesus Is Brought Before the Authorities,
Jn. 18:20–24, 32–34

Jesus, having been betrayed by Judas, was arrested, bound, and taken before the ecclesiastical authorities. There he was unbound and informally questioned by Annas. He previously had been the high priest and still was the leading influence amongst the Jews. Annas questioned Jesus about his teaching and the nature of his disciples. It seems he hoped to uncover some evidence of revolutionary activity.

Jesus answered, "I have spoken openly to the world; I have always taught in synagogues and the temple, where all the Jews come together. I have said nothing in secret. Why do you ask me? Ask those who heard what I said to them; they know what I said." When he had said this, one of the police standing by struck Jesus in the face, saying, "Is that how you answer the high priest?" Jesus answered, "If I have spoken wrongly, testify to the wrong. But if I have spoken rightly, why do you strike me?"

Jesus' two questions exemplify the double meaning of the question, 'Why?' In the first instance, his focus was on *the purpose* of being asked. In law, no one was required to give evidence against themselves. It was up to Jesus' accusers to charge him and, if necessary, to call witnesses against him. As he correctly pointed out, he had always spoken openly to everyone. He had always taught in public places. There was nothing secret about his teaching. What then was *their purpose* in asking him about his teaching and his disciples?

The authorities had no answer other than to insult Jesus by slapping his face!

In putting his second question, the focus changed. What now was being asked was *how did it come about* that they should treat him so? There was no one to testify against him. He claimed always to have spoken rightly. How could they possibly justify insulting him this way? Again, the authorities had no answer.

The informal interrogation over, Jesus was again bound and sent before a gathering of the Sanhedrin under the presidency of Caiaphas. He was the high priest and son-in-law of Annas. They formally confirmed the decision already made at the irregular meeting in the house of Annas. * Jesus was then led to Pilate, the civil authority, who came out of his headquarters to enquire what accusation the Sanhedrin brought against Jesus. Unsure of their case the temple officers hesitated to specify the charge. When Pilate declined to proceed, they at last admitted that they sought the death penalty for Jesus.

Pilate entered the headquarters again, summoned Jesus, and asked him, "Are you the King of the Jews?" Jesus answered, "Do you ask this on your own, or did others tell you about me?"

In this private interview with the Procurator, there may well have been a note of surprise in Pilate's opening question. Jesus' appearance and demeanour did not suggest a militant revolutionary leader. The allegation was, however, that Jesus had assumed the title King of the Jews. As a civil title, this was far more threatening politically than the theocratic title, King of Israel. Pilate, therefore, took it seriously.

Jesus' counter-question troubled Pilate. It challenged whether Pilate was worried about his own authority being compromised or, alternatively, about accepting at face value an accusation by the Jewish leaders which had all the hallmarks of being unfounded and malicious.

Jesus' question hit home. Hastily, Pilate declared his indifference to Jewish affairs and enquired instead what Jesus had done to provoke such hostility from the temple authorities. Jesus carefully explained that his kingdom 'was not from this world'. It was, therefore, no threat to Pilate or to Rome.

Finding no fault with Jesus Pilate sought to diffuse the situation, but it was to no avail. Ultimately, and despite the formidable defence presented by Jesus' questions, Pilate handed him over to be crucified.

*The dislocation of John's original text makes it difficult to be precise about this order of events.

----

103. For Whom Are You Looking?
The Risen Lord Appears to Mary Magdalene,
Jn. 20:14–15

Mary Magdalene had come to Jesus' tomb early on Sunday morning. Seeing the stone had been removed she ran to Peter, and another 'whom Jesus loved', to tell them of the suspicious circumstances. They ran to investigate but finding only the linen wrappings carefully arranged they withdrew. Mary remained outside, weeping. When eventually she looked in, the tomb was no longer empty. Two angels were present. On seeing her, they asked why she was weeping. Briefly, she retold her story that somebody had taken away her Lord and she did not know where they had laid him.

When she had said this, she turned around and saw Jesus standing there, but she did not know that it was Jesus. Jesus said to her, "Woman, why are you weeping? For whom are you looking?"

These two questions appear to be Jesus' first words after his resurrection. His initial question repeats exactly the one put to Mary by the angels in the tomb. The meaning here is, "What has brought about these tears?" The angels seemed not to have understood the cause of Mary's grief. By contrast, Jesus' second question reveals his immediate appreciation of Mary's tears. They arose from her loss of a loved one. So, Jesus asks not, "*What* are you looking for?" but, "*For whom* are you looking?"

His question is assumptive. It takes for granted that Mary is searching not for some precious object, but for someone very dear. It is a sensitive question and reveals both Jesus' insight into Mary's sorrow and his deep understanding of the human condition.

----

104. Have You Believed Because You Have Seen Me?

Jesus Appears to Thomas, Jn. 20:20–29

On the morning of the day when Jesus' tomb was discovered to be empty, the disciples 'for fear of the Jews' locked the door of the house in which they were gathered. Thomas was not with them. When, subsequently, he was told by the disciples that Jesus had stood amongst them Thomas replied that he could not believe them unless he saw for himself the wounds of Jesus' crucifixion.

A week later his disciples were again in the house, and Thomas was with them. Although the doors were shut, Jesus came and stood among them and said, "Peace be with you." Then he said to Thomas, "Put your finger here and see my hands. Reach out your hand and put it in my side. Do not doubt but believe." Thomas answered him, "My Lord and my God!" Jesus said to him, "Have you believed because you have seen me? Blessed are those who have not seen and yet have believed."

It was at once clear to Thomas from Jesus' words that he knew of the doubts Thomas had held previously, and what he had said. Jesus had read his heart. There was, therefore, no longer any need to touch the wounds. It was enough for Thomas to be gently rebuked and in all adoration to confess not just, 'My Lord', but 'My God!'

Jesus' response exemplifies an unusual form of a question. It is neither rhetorical nor a simple request for information. It is a form Jesus sometimes used as halfway between a statement and a question, almost a tag-question. "You have believed because you have seen me, haven't you?" It establishes the truth of a situation. Here, however, Jesus also uses it to lead into what many acknowledge as the greatest of all Beatitudes, "Blessed are those who have not seen and yet have believed."

----

105. You Have No Fish, Have You?
The Risen Lord Appears by the Sea, Jn. 21:4-5

John's gospel records that the risen Jesus appeared on the first day of the week, in the early morning to Mary Magdalene, in the evening to the disciples, and eight days later again to the disciples when Thomas was with them. Now, for a third time, Jesus appears to seven of the disciples by the Sea of Tiberias. They were just returning from an unsuccessful fishing trip.

Just after daybreak, Jesus stood on the beach; but the disciples did not know that it was Jesus. Jesus said to them, "Children, you have no fish, have you?" They answered him, "No."

Interestingly, although the disciples had seen the risen Lord twice before they did not recognise him even when he spoke to them. It seems that only when Jesus chose to reveal himself did he become recognisable. Neither Mary Magdalene nor the two disciples on the road to Emmaus had recognised Jesus initially.

Jesus' address to the disciples is unexpectedly familiar and his leading question is in tag form. It anticipates a negative answer, and this having been established it opened the way for Jesus to direct the disciples to cast their net on the other side of the boat. When, unexpectedly, they then caught a great many fish, 'that disciple whom Jesus loved' realised who Jesus was and told the others. Peter, jumping into the sea went to greet him. The other disciples came in the boat dragging the nets.

As so often was the case the purpose of Jesus' question extended beyond a simple enquiry. Here it was not just a friendly call, "Any luck?" It was the means of making himself known by events.

223

106. Do You Love Me?
The Risen Lord and Peter, Jn. 21:15-17

It was just after daybreak by the Sea of Tiberius. Jesus had appeared for the third time to some of his disciples. He was standing on the beach. They had been fishing about one hundred yards offshore.

They first realised it was Jesus only when, in response to his guidance, they suddenly and unexpectedly began to catch many fish in their nets. They came ashore and Jesus invited them to eat with him around a charcoal fire alight on the beach. Although they knew it was the Lord, they feared to question him.

When they had finished breakfast, Jesus said to Simon Peter, "Simon son of John, do you love me more than these?" He said to him, "Yes, Lord; you know that I love you." Jesus said to him, "Feed my lambs." A second time he said to him, "Simon, son of John, do you love me?" He said to him, "Yes, Lord; you know that I love you." Jesus said to him, "Tend my sheep." He said to him the third time, "Simon, son of John, do you love me?" Peter felt hurt because he said to him the third time, "Do you love me?" And he said to him, "Lord, you know everything; you know that I love you." Jesus said to him, "Feed my sheep."

It is not clear in Jesus' first question to whom or to what he is referring when he asks Peter, "do you love me *more than these?*" It is thought most likely that he meant, "more than your fellow companions?" It is not improbable, however, that he may also have been referring to the surrounding nets and boats as symbols of Peter's life as a fisherman.

The obvious focus of the narrative is on Peter's love for Jesus. There is no mention of Peter's belief in Jesus as the Christ, or Peter's willingness to lay down his life for Jesus as a disciple. The dialogue is solely about 'love' as that word is understood between them.

Commentators debate the use in this text of the two Greek verbs, *agapan* and *philein,* both of which can be transliterated 'to love'. In the New Testament, the first represents a higher form of unconditional, self-giving love. The second represents a more general, friendly, affectionate love. It is not always easy to distinguish the shades of meaning between these two and no sharp distinction is made between them in older commentaries.

Modern exegetes, however, often accept that in the present context the difference is significant, and that Peter does not presume to claim the higher form of love. Thus, when Jesus puts his first two questions, and we might presume a short interval between all three questions, he uses the word *agapas* for 'love'. Peter, on the other hand, replies using the word *philo* for 'love'. When Jesus asks the third time, "do you love me?" he uses the word *phileis,* Peter's own description of his love, thus acknowledging Peter's uncertainty in over-committing himself.

Possibly it was because Peter remembered how he had previously denied Jesus three times that he was hurt by the re-wording of Jesus' third question. Perhaps Peter felt that once more he had failed Jesus at a defining moment. Characteristically, he appeals to Jesus' deep perception of human nature and trusts him to understand.

In this touching narrative, Jesus' third question seems to reveal a hope unrealised. Peter, of all his disciples, might have been the one to commit himself to that higher form of love, which reflects God's divine love for all humankind. Seemingly, it was not to be!

----

107. Follow Me!

Concerning Jesus' Last Instruction to Peter, Jn. 21:20–22

Following the dialogue between Jesus and Peter on the beach by the Sea of Tiberius, Jesus had referred briefly to the possible martyrdom of Peter at some future date (vv. 18–19). He then said to Peter, "Follow me."

As they both moved away from the other six Peter's attention was drawn to a movement behind him.

Peter turned and saw the disciple whom Jesus loved following them; he was the one who had reclined next to Jesus at the supper and had said, "Lord, who is it that is going to betray you?" When Peter saw him, he said to Jesus, "Lord, what about him?" Jesus said to him, "If it is my will that he remains until I come, what is that to you? Follow me!"

Traditionally, it is thought that the one following after Peter and Jesus, although uninvited, was the apostle John, son of Zebedee. Peter, mindful perhaps of his own martyrdom as just predicted by Jesus, asks what is to be the future fate of John. His enquiry is met with a sharp reproof in the form of a rhetorical counter-question. This is not easy to interpret.

Jesus could have said simply, something like, "That is not for you to ask." It could be, however, that the mention of John "remaining until Jesus comes" is an oblique reference to the nearness of the *Parousia*. If so, then implicit in Jesus' rebuke may be the thought that whatever is the Divine Will for the destiny of others it is no concern of Peter's! It is sufficient that he is clear about his own duty. Jesus, therefore, repeats his instruction, "Follow me!"

It is interesting that in the last Gospel the last recorded words of Jesus, which offer an essential precept for Christian life, arise typically from the rabbinical use of a rhetorical counter-question.

The Acts of the Apostles
108. Why Do You Persecute Me?
Saul's Conversion on the Road to Damascus, Acts 9:3–5

Prior to his conversion to Christianity Saul of Tarsus ravaged the early Church in Jerusalem and Judaea. He also approved the stoning to death of Stephen, "a man full of faith and the Holy Spirit" chosen to be a deacon. Saul then obtained letters from the high priest at the Sanhedrin in Jerusalem authorising him to search the synagogues at Damascus for Christians and return them bound to Jerusalem.

Now as he was going along and approaching Damascus, suddenly a light from heaven flashed around him. He fell to the ground and heard a voice saying to him, "Saul, Saul, why do you persecute me?" He asked, "Who are you, Lord?" The reply came, "I am Jesus, whom you are persecuting." ("It hurts you to kick against the goads." 26:14).

There are three slightly different versions of Saul's conversion, (9:3–5, 22:4–16, 26:12–15). In each narrative, it is clear that Saul believed the voice he heard was that of Jesus. Others present were said to have heard the sound of a voice but not the words that were spoken.

How this narrative is received depends very largely upon the extent to which it is accepted that divine action can enter into human affairs. It is a report of an extremely personal religious experience in one whose psychological state at the time is open to conjecture. The possibility that Saul was hallucinating is beyond the remit of this note.

It is thought that Saul never met or saw Jesus. It is interesting, therefore, that Jesus' question refers only to himself and not to the Christians and disciples whom Paul had been persecuting. It is also thought that Jesus' question may be an early reference to the Church as the Body of Christ.

Regarding Jesus' use of, '*Why*', two subsidiary questions require consideration. "What has *caused* you to persecute me?" and "What do you *hope to achieve* by persecuting me?" Both questions would strike home with Saul.

The stress on the first of these probably is minimal. Saul's background was well known. He was a Jew of the tribe of Benjamin. He had inherited Roman citizenship from his father and had come to Jerusalem to study Law and Tradition under Gamaliel.

Saul's training and formative background were thoroughly Jewish and, as a rising young man devoted to Pharisaic Judaism, he exhibited a very natural zeal for knowledge of the Law as the pathway to righteousness. It was intolerable to him, therefore, that Christians should presume to be a Messianic community or preach the crucified Jesus to be Messiah. This was considered to be dismissive of Judaism as the religion of the nation, and of Yahweh as the exclusive God of Israel.

Saul also was infuriated by the radical teaching of Stephen who had prophesied against the Temple. He had driven a clear wedge between the two faiths so that Christianity was no longer compatible with traditional Judaism. Predictably, Saul's response was violent and prompt!

It is probable that Jesus' question chiefly concerned Saul's *purpose* in persecuting the Church. Modern texts omit verse 5b although it appears later in 26:14. This is an ancient proverb that offers a clue to the answer Jesus expected. The goad was a light wooden pole at one end of which was an iron spike to prick the oxen during farming.

The more the oxen kicked against the goad the more it pricked them! The more one resisted the more one suffered from the resistance! The proverbial message was that it was senseless to resist a power superior to one's own.

This proverb seems to fit what was happening to Saul. He had been profoundly affected by the martyrdom of Stephen. Also, perhaps, he had found himself secretly troubled that Stephen and these Christians had discovered something true.

Was it just possible that they had been right all the time? Now, suddenly, in a blinding flash, Jesus' question disclosed to Saul that in his violent actions he had been striving to hide from himself the persistent pricking of his conscience. He had been trying to suppress the innermost suspicion of his heart that he had mistaken the true path to righteousness. As a result, he had not only persecuted innocent Christians he had persecuted Messiah himself!

Jesus' question came to Saul as an overwhelming revelation of divine activity!

Jesus' Questions Examined in Chronological Order

Table 2. A Brief Chronology of Events in which Jesus Questions are Recorded. *

The Childhood of Jesus.

In the Temple at Judaea (Lk. 2:41–50).

Early Galilean Ministry.

(Initially around Nazareth. Subsequently around Capernaum.
Mark records various early mission tours, 1:15–7:23.)
The sermon on the mount (Mt. 7:15–20).
The first 'Sabbath' disputes (Mk. 2:1–12).
(On fasting. Mk. 2:18–22).
(Two blind men healed. Mt. 9:27–31).
(Further Sabbath disputes. Mk. 2:23–28, 3:1–6).
The sermon on the plain (Lk. 6:17–49).
Jesus' tribute to John (Lk. 7:24–35).
The Beelzebub controversy (Mk. 3:22–26, 3:31–35).
Kingdom parables (Mk. 4:1–9, 21–28, 30–32, Mt. 13:51–52).
Calming the storm (Mk. 4:35–41).
(Further preaching tours. Mk. 5:1–43)
(Exorcism and healings. Mk. 5:1–20, 21–43).
(Rejection in Nazareth. Mk. 6:1).

Middle Galilean Ministry

(Feeding the five thousand. Mk. 6:30–44).
Jesus walks on water (Mt. 14:22–33).
(Teaching on defilement. Mk. 7:1–23, Mt. 15:1–20).
(Feeding the four thousand. Mk. 8:1–10).

Demands for signs (Mk. 8:11–13, 14–21).

(Healing a blind man. Mk. 8:22–26).

Caesarea Philippi (Mk. 8:27–33, 34–38).

(The Transfiguration. Mk. 9:1–8, 9–13).

An epileptic boy healed (Mk. 9:14–29).

Temple tax (Mt. 17:24–27).

(Arguments about greatness. Mk. 9:31, 33–37).

The disciples must retain 'their salt' (Mk. 9:47–50).

Late Galilean Ministry.

(Commissioning the seventy. Lk. 9:51, 10:1–12).

Criticism of Chorazin, Bethsaida, and Capernaum (Lk. 10:13–15).

(The lawyers question. Lk. 10:25–28).

(The Good Samaritan. Lk. 10:29–37).

(On persistence with prayer. Lk. 11:11–13).

(Disputes with the Pharisees. Lk. 11:37–41).

(The disciples precious in God's sight. Lk. 12:3–12).

(Parable of the rich fool. Lk. 12:13–21).

The disciples must trust in God's providence and remain alert (Lk, 12:22–31, 35–48).

The people should read the signs and repent (Lk. 12:51–57).

(A crippled woman healed. Lk. 13:10–17).

The Departure from Galilee, and the Road to Jerusalem.

[Mk (10:1–10:46) and Mt (19:1–20:29) suggest about two weeks.

Lk (13:34–35–19:1) suggests far longer, perhaps several months.

There is no main centre in this section.]

(On divorce. Mk. 10:1–12).

(A rich young man. Mk. 10:17–22).

Positions of honour (Mk. 10:32, 36–38).

(The man with dropsy. Lk. 13:34–35, 14:1–6)

Preparation for discipleship (Lk. 14:28–32).

(Joy at finding those who were lost. Lk. 15:3–10).

The dishonest manager (Lk. 16:1–13).

Kingdom parables (Lk. 17:11–19).

(Healing ten lepers. 17:11–19).
Doubt about his mission? (Lk. 18:1–8).

Arriving in Jerusalem.

Acknowledging Messianic status (Mt. 21:10–17).
(At Jericho. Mk. 10, Mt. 20:29, Lk. 19:1).
(Blind Bartimaeus. Mk. 10:46–52).
(At Bethpage and Bethany. Mk. 11:1, Lk. 19:29, Mt. 21:1).

The Last Week in Jerusalem.

Cleansing the Temple (Mk. 11:15–19).
(A question of authority. Mk. 11:27–33).
Parable of the two sons (Mt. 21:28–32).
Parable of the vineyard (Mk. 12:1–12).
(Taxes to the Emperor. Mk. 12:13–17).
(On resurrection. Mk. 12:18–27).
(Concerning David's son. Mk. 12:35–37).
(The seven woes. Mt. 23:17–19).
Prediction of the destruction of the Temple (Mk. 13:1–4).
(The synoptic apocalypse. Mt. 24:4–36, Mk. 13:5–37, Lk 21:8–36).

The Passion Narratives.

Jesus was anointed with costly ointment (Mk. 14:3–9, Lk. 7:36–50).
(The last supper.)
The arrest (Mk. 14:43–50, Lk. 22:47–53, Mt. 26:51–54).
(The crucifixion.)

Resurrection Appearances.

*This chronology reflects the broad general agreement of the synoptic gospels. It is difficult to match the chronology of John's gospel to this pattern.

The events bracketed record questions related chiefly to incidental events. Those not bracketed record questions which reveal Jesus' train of thought as events unfold.

The synoptic gospels do not present an exact record of Jesus' life. Each gospel offers its own perspective. The synoptic gospels, however, agree broadly about the chronology of Jesus' ministry. Table 2 summarises the order of events in which Jesus' questions are recorded and this offers the opportunity to review his questions consecutively.

It is clear from the earlier study of the gospels that some of Jesus' questions reflect the deep tidal pull of history while others concern just the surface waves of incidental events. When the 'deeper' questions are considered in consecutive order, we obtain some idea of Jesus' train of thought as events unfold.

Luke records Jesus at the age of twelve sitting amongst the teachers in the Temple at Jerusalem asking them questions. His startling question to Mary and Joseph, who had been searching for him for three days, reveals an early and extraordinary relationship both to his parents and to the Temple as his 'Father's house'.

Subsequently, we learn little of Jesus' life until about the age of thirty when he visited Judaea in preparation for his ministry. There he was publicly baptised by John in the River Jordan and afterwards spent forty days in the wilderness preparing himself internally for his mission. (The Gospels record no questions at this time.) Probably following the arrest and imprisonment of John, Jesus returned to Nazareth in Galilee where his activities are usually subdivided into an early, middle, and late Galilean period.

Initially, Jesus visited many of the neighbouring towns around Capernaum teaching in the synagogues. Several times he returned to Nazareth. In this early section, his questions suggest a considerable degree of confidence in both his authority and his expectations. They warn against the danger of being led astray by false prophets, claim authority as the Son of Man, and present his (temporary) association with his disciples as a time of Joy.

In the early phases of 'the Sabbath battle', they establish his authority to quote scripture, discomfort the Pharisees and challenge their biblical fundamentalism. In the Sermon on the Plain, his questions emphasise the importance of loving one's neighbour, of removing one's own faults before criticising others, and of being confident in his teaching. Subsequently, they are used to pay respect to the Baptist as a fine spiritual leader, and later, in the Beelzebub controversy, to successfully protect himself against accusations of 'being possessed'. At this time also, Jesus' questions make clear that he is not to be defined by his family relationships.

Following a series of parables, his questions reveal the first glimmering of surprise that his disciples have not always understood his teaching. "Do you understand this parable?" he asks. "Have you understood all this?" Plainly, it is important to Jesus that they should understand, to safeguard the future of his mission. After stilling the storm on the Sea of Galilee, again he questions, "Have you still no faith?"

At the close of this early section, Mark records a preaching tour during which Jesus' questions reflect his perception of illness, an innate sense of his healing power, and his occasional extraordinary foreknowledge of events. The tour ends at Nazareth where he is rejected. Thereafter he centres on Capernaum as his home.

In the middle section of his Galilean ministry, following the feeding of the five thousand, Jesus' questions gradually reveal an increasing disquiet that his mission is not being understood. Thus, at the miracle of walking on water he questions the disciples, "You of little faith, why did you doubt?"

And again, after teaching on defilement, "Do you also fail to understand?" or "Are you still without understanding?" After feeding the four thousand, he argues with the Pharisees, "Why do this generation ask for a sign?" Subsequently, he also vents his frustration on the disciples in their boat, "Do you still not perceive or understand? Are your hearts hardened? Do you have eyes, and fail to see? Do you have ears and fail to hear?"

Up to this point, Jesus' activities have focussed largely on mission tours, healing the people, teaching about the Kingdom, and encouraging his disciples. Now there is a significant change. His questions suggest an increasing sense of urgency and focus more upon himself. At Caesarea Philippi, he asks, "Who do people say that I am? Who do you say that I am?" Frustration and irritation with his contemporaries become more apparent.

What will it profit them to gain the whole world, and yet lose their life? And following the transfiguration, again he questions them, "You faithless generation. How much longer must I be among you? How much longer must I put up with you?" Thereafter, with his disciples in Galilee, his questions re-emphasise his status as the Son of God, also the Temple as his Father's house. The disciples must retain their 'salt' if they are to safeguard his mission in the future.

The late Galilean period is largely given to preparation for the final visit to Jerusalem. Jesus appoints seventy others to go in pairs to every town he intends to visit to prepare for his coming. His questions reveal a previous disappointment at his reception in Chorazin, Bethsaida and Capernaum. The prevailing belief seems to be that the Kingdom is at hand and time for preparation is short. Questions warn the disciples to keep awake and be ready to greet their master when he comes. They must remain alert for the unexpected. The people must realise that their time for decision is imminent. Jesus questions charge them to read the signs and repent.

After leaving Galilee and taking the road to Jerusalem, Mark records Jesus' question to James and John. They plainly had failed to comprehend what lay ahead and he asks them, "Are you able to drink of the cup that I drink, or be baptised with the baptism that I am baptised with?"

Luke, in his longer narrative, records questions, which emphasise the need to prepare for discipleship, and for the future. If people are to be trusted with the riches of the Kingdom, they must prove themselves honest in worldly matters. As disciples in the Kingdom, they are expected to know what God requires of them, and to do it! "And yet", asks Jesus, "when the Son of Man comes, will he find faith on earth?"

As they arrive at Jerusalem, Jesus' questions openly acknowledge the Messianic cries of the children. When he cleansed the Temple, he again refers to it in terms of his Father's house. He warns the authorities in Israel that they will be destroyed and replaced. To his disciples, he predicts the destruction of the Temple. The 'little apocalypse' graphically describes the extraordinary events and calamities which are expected to bring to an end the world as they know it and herald the coming of the Son of Man.

In the Passion narratives, two days before the Passover in the house of Simon the leper, Jesus' question clearly foreshadows his impending death and burial. Later, at his arrest in Gethsemane, again his questions to the crowd indicate the inevitability of the Passion. "Do you think that I cannot appeal to my Father, and he will at once send me more than twelve legions of angels? But how then would the scriptures be fulfilled which say it must happen this way?"

As all these 'deep' questions unfold we are helped to imagine Jesus' sense of mission, not just in terms of his divine authority but also in terms of its importance; and then, with the passage of time, his anxieties lest it should fail. We can feel his sense of urgency, his uncertainties, his frustration, and his acceptance of the Passion as inevitable. In this chronology of questions, we perceive the drama of his acceptance and fulfilment of the role of the 'suffering servant'.

Jesus' Use of Questions and What They Reveal About Him

Jesus' use of questions was far more extensive than just seeking information. Some are obscure and some difficult to understand (Jn. 11:7–11, Lk. 14:28–32, 15:3–10). In general, however, his questions were effective tools, and an overview suggests that they fall naturally into two broad groups. In one group, the questions are typically straightforward and used to promote his teaching and ministry. In the other group, the questions are more forceful and aggressive and are used to discomfort or discredit his critics and opponents.

The First Group

Within the first group, it is quickly apparent that of the many questions Jesus asked, relatively few are really 'open' in the sense of inviting opinion or thoughtful comment. In general, Jesus seems not to have sought the advice of others. Certainly, he sometimes asked questions inviting a slightly longer form of reply. "Why were you searching for me? Did you not know I must be in my Father's house?" (Lk. 2:48–49). "What is it you want me to do for you?" (Mk. 10:36–39). "What did Moses command you?" (Mk. 10:1–12).
On the road to Emmaus, "What things?" (Lk. 24:13–27). In several narratives, however, questions that at first seem to be 'open' are often cut short. Sometimes this is because the available options are restricted. For example, when Jesus asks, "What do you think?" (Mt. 17:24–29, Mt. 21:28–32) only one of two options are possible thereby curtailing the probable answer.

On other occasions, Jesus simply gives the person no time to reply. In discussion with Nicodemus (Jn. 3:10–17), Jesus asks, "Are you a teacher of Israel yet you do not understand these things?" In addressing the Jews, he asks, "Why do I speak to you at all?" (Jn. 8:25f). When debating with the Temple authorities, "What will the owner of the vineyard do?" (Mk. 12:1–12). In each instance, although the question appears to be 'open' it is largely rhetorical, and no answer is expected. Overall, the impression is quite strong that Jesus' use of questions in this group was usually constructed if not strictly in a closed form, then certainly in such a way as to retain control of the conversation. Perhaps this was a typically Rabbinical approach to debate. Alternatively, perhaps it stemmed from Jesus' innate sense of divine authority.

The different circumstances in which his ordinary questions were used include: -

To Establish Biblical Precedents.

Jesus often used a question to introduce a biblical passage. He then would apply this in support of his argument. In driving out the traders from the Temple, for example he asks, "Is it not written?" and draws their attention to passages from Isaiah and Jeremiah, albeit adapted to his needs (Mk. 11:15–17). When arguing with representatives of the Sanhedrin he asks, "Have you not read this scripture?" and draws their attention to Psalm 118 (Mk. 12:1–12).

Similarly, when the chief priests and scribes were angry at the children crying out, "Hosanna to the Son of David," Jesus puts the question, "Yes; have you never read?" and quotes from the Psalms (Mt. 21:15–16). On other occasions, Jesus used the technique to establish a notable exception to a general rule. Thus, when Pharisees charged his disciples with breaking the Law by plucking heads of grain as they walked through the cornfields, Jesus cites the occasion when David and his companions ate the bread of the Presence in the Temple (Mk. 2:23–26).

To Introduce His Teaching and/or Illustrative Parables.

Frequently Jesus used a question to introduce his teaching. So, when a young lawyer asks what he should do to inherit eternal life Jesus replies, "What is written in the Law? What do you read there?" (Lk. 10:25–28) and the lawyer correctly quotes from Deuteronomy and Leviticus. When teaching his disciples about the importance of humility and service, he asks, "Who is greater, the one who is at the table or the one who serves?" (Lk. 22:24–30).

And after his famous parable of The Good Samaritan, Jesus drives home his lesson with the question, "Which of these three, do you think, was a neighbour to the man who fell into the hands of the robber?" Also integral to Jesus' teaching was his use of questions to introduce an illustrative parable. "To what shall I compare the people of this generation?" he asks, which leads to the parable of children playing in the marketplace (Lk. 7:31–33). Or, when his disciples were uncertain about his teaching on watchfulness, he asks, "Who then is the faithful and prudent manager etc.?" which leads to a further parable on trustworthy and untrustworthy domestic managers (Lk. 12:42–47).

Occasionally his questions also hint at some disappointment that his teaching and mission may not have been as successful as he hoped. In particular, they reveal his disappointment at the response of Chorazin, Bethsaida, and Capernaum (Lk. 10:13–15). And on another occasion, one can almost sense the unhappiness in his voice when he asks his disciples, "Do you also wish to go away?" (Jn. 6:66–70).

To Re-Direct a Discussion.

Sometimes, Jesus would use a question to re-direct a debate, notably when he thought there was a more important aspect to discuss. Thus, on an occasion when ritual fasting dominated the talk, he broadened the discussion with the tag-question, "The wedding guests cannot fast while the bridegroom is with them, can they?" (Mk. 2:18–20). Similarly, following the transfiguration, when his disciples were focussed on Elijah, Jesus transfers their attention with the question, "How then is it written about the Son of Man, that he is to go through many sufferings and be treated with contempt?" (Mk. 9:9–13).

To Precipitate a Sign.

It was not often that Jesus performed a 'sign' (miracle) simply to establish his identity or authority. On the few occasions, when he deemed it necessary, however, the sign was introduced with a question. At Capernaum, for example, where his authority to forgive sins was silently questioned by the scribes, he asks, "Which is easier, to say to the paralytic, 'Your sins are forgiven', or to say, 'Stand up and take you mat and walk'?" Then, without waiting for a reply he cured the man (Mk. 2:1–12).

Also, by the sea of Tiberius, he began with the tag-question, "Children, you have no fish, have you?" And so began the miracle of the fishes by which Jesus secretly made himself known to the disciples (Jn. 21:4–8).

The Second Group

Within the second group of questions Jesus always was very protective of his disciples and readily would use a counter-question to deflect criticism away from them. So, for example, when the Pharisees criticised the disciples for not washing their hands before they ate, Jesus sharply countered with the question, "And why do you break the commandment of God for the sake of your tradition?" He then attacked the Pharisees for their hypocrisy (Mt. 15:1–9).

If Jesus himself was challenged, he was equally adept at using questions to turn defence into attack. Thus, when the authorities sought to kill him because he healed on the Sabbath and because he called God his own father, his question is clear and direct, "How can you believe when you accept glory from one another and do not seek the glory that comes from the one who alone is God?" (Jn. 5:42–47). In a similar manner, he often would use questions effectively to rob his critics of their initiative.

So, when the chief priests and scribes challenged his authority within the Temple they were forced into silence by his question, "Did the baptism of John come from heaven, or was it of human origin?" (Mt. 11:27–33). And then, in the synagogue when Jesus was watched to see if he would cure a man on the Sabbath so that they might accuse him, they could not reply to his question, "Is it lawful to do good or to do harm on the Sabbath, to save life or to kill?" (Mk. 3:1–5).

Or again, on a Sabbath in the house of a leader of the Pharisees, they silently watched Jesus to see if he would heal a man with dropsy. So, he challenged them with the question, "If one of you has a child or an ox that has fallen into a well, will you not immediately pull it out on a Sabbath day?" Once more they had no reply. With each question, Jesus forcefully exposed the shortcomings in the authority of his opponents, and they were argued into silence.

Even more aggressive was Jesus' use of questions when he allowed his frustration and anger to surface. Then he could be quite vehement and unhesitatingly direct. "You brood of vipers" he threw at the Pharisees, "How can you speak good things, when you are evil?" (Mt. 12:43–37).

Or, in the seven 'woes', again when denouncing Pharisaic hypocrisy, "You snakes, you brood of vipers!" he said. "How can you escape being sentenced to hell?" (Mt. 23:29–33). And on another occasion when Pharisees expressed amazement that he did not first wash before dinner, Jesus forcefully challenged their hypocrisy with, "You fools! Did not the one who made the outside make the inside also?" (Lk. 11:37–41). Also, he was equally scathing in his indictment of the religious leaders on the matter of swearing oaths in the Temple. "You blind fools!" he said. "For which is greater, the gold or the sanctuary that has made the gold sacred?" (Mt. 23:16–19).

While it is the case that Jesus' aggressive use of questions usually arose in response to challenges made to him, sometimes he would take the opportunity to use a question unexpectedly, though no less forcibly, to accuse his opponents. For example, having successfully defended himself against a challenge to his authority in the Temple, he then cleverly interested the chief priests, the scribes, and the elders with the 'Parable of the Vineyard'. At the end, when his listeners were least expecting it, he asks, "Have you not read this scripture: 'The stone that the builders rejected has become the cornerstone; this was the Lord's doing, and it is amazing in our eyes'?" (Mk. 12:1–12). Suddenly his listeners were conscious that Jesus had told the parable against them and, as before, they were forced into silence because of the crowds!

Although the Gospels tell us much about how Jesus used his questions, they tell us little of how he delivered them, his use of dramatic pauses, the tone of his voice, or his display of mood. There is much we are left to imagine. Nevertheless, it seems clear that when occasion demanded he could furnish his questions with a real sense of oratory. We have only to think, for example, of his wonderful crescendo of questions when speaking about John the Baptist.

Addressing the crowd Jesus asks, "What did you go out into the wilderness to look at? What did you go out to see? Someone dressed in fine clothes? What did you go out to see? A prophet? Yes, I tell you, and more than a prophet." (Mt. 11:7–10). Our imagination is fired to add Jesus' inflection of voice, his pause between each question, his command of the situation.

Or, on another occasion, when three times Jesus poignantly asked Peter, "Simon, son of John, do you love me more than these?" Surely, we cannot fail to imagine both a gentleness in Jesus' voice and a quiet pause between each question, especially the last.

How Jesus' Questions Reveal Something of Himself as a Person

What is meant by 'a person' sometimes excites comments. Here it is used as a term of value to describe how someone evaluates their life in relation to themselves, their neighbour, their environment, and God. In this section, we examine Jesus' personhood through his questions.

Jesus' Relationship to Himself

Exploring Jesus' relationship to himself immediately raises the Christological dilemma of two natures in one person. So far as we know, Jesus never spoke of his incarnation. Nevertheless, the Gospels are at pains to present him as both human and divine.

Expressions of his ordinary human trait include fatigue and thirst (Jn. 4:6–7, 19:28), hunger after fasting (Mt. 4:2), emotions such as love (Jn. 20:2), joy (Lk. 10:21), sorrow (Mt. 26:38), and anger (Mk. 3:4–5). Many of his questions, particularly in Mark, exemplify Jesus' ordinary human approach to everyday affairs (cf. the Introduction).

Jesus' divine nature also is portrayed in many ways, notably in John 14. Sometimes we have Jesus' own words as in the seven 'I am' sayings. Sometimes we have the words of others. The Centurion at the crucifixion (Mk. 15:39) said, "Truly, this man is God's son."

However, it is in Jesus' questions that we catch a direct glimpse of the recognition within himself of his divine nature. In the narrative of Jairus' daughter, for example (Lk. 8:49–56), Jesus asks the people, "Why do you make a commotion and weep? The child is not dead but sleeping." Plainly, though he had not seen the child, Jesus had clear foreknowledge of what was about to happen.

Similarly, when he asks Peter (Jn. 13;38), "Will you lay down your life for me?" Jesus clearly foresaw that Peter would deny Him three times before the cock crowed. And again, in the narrative of the crowd where a woman secretly touched the fringe of Jesus' cloak in the belief, she would be healed (Mk. 5:25–34) Jesus knew immediately that divine power had gone out from him. Nevertheless, in a very ordinary sense, he asked, "Who touched my clothes?" for he did not know who had touched him!

From Luke's Gospel, we learn that even as a young boy Jesus was self-conscious of being in some way 'extra-ordinary'. Thus, when his distracted parents were searching for him and found him in the Temple sitting among the teachers his question, "Why were you searching for me? Did you not know that I must be in my Father's house?" suggests an early realisation of his divine nature (Lk. 2:48–49). It was not until some twenty years later, however, following his baptism by John that we see Jesus truly assured of his divine nature.

By then he had developed the authority to forgive sins and perform 'signs' (Mk. 2:3–12), to teach in the synagogue and the Temple, and to interpret the scriptures (Lk. 4:14–21, Mk. 10:1–12, Jn. 7:28–30). Otherwise, it seems he did not see his sense of divine authority extending to ordinary everyday events. So, when asked for advice on a division of family inheritance he replied quite naturally, "Friend, who sent me to be a judge or arbiter over you?" (Lk. 12:13–31).

It appears to have been important to Jesus that his self-assurance of divine authority was recognised by others. Indeed, when it was not acknowledged it appears to have been a cause of personal frustration and perhaps even exasperation. So, in his sermon on the plain, he says to the crowd, "Why do you call me 'Lord, Lord,' and do not do what I tell you?" (Lk. 6:46–49). Or, in his argument with the Jews when he had made it clear to them that he came from God, "Why do you not understand what I say?" (Jn. 8:43).

As mentioned above, sometimes Jesus' questions revealed a clear foreknowledge of forthcoming events. Other of his questions suggest that this was true also of his own destiny. An early foreshadowing of his death, for example, occurs when, in Levi's house during a discussion on ritual fasting, Jesus asks, "The wedding guests cannot fast while the bridegroom is with them, can they? The day will come when the bridegroom is taken away from them, and then they will fast on that day" (Mk. 2:18, 21).

Also, in Mark's Gospel (after 8:27–29) we see that the emphasis of Jesus' teaching transfers from his message to the significance of himself as a person. This becomes particularly notable towards the end of his life when his questions seem to reveal a clear foreknowledge of his forthcoming passion. Thus, he asks James and John, "Are you able to drink the cup that I drink, or be baptised with the baptism that I am baptised with?" (Mk. 10:38).

And in the house of Simon the leper where a woman anoints Jesus' head with a costly ointment and others were angry, he says to them, "Let her alone; why do you trouble her? She has done what she could; she has anointed my body beforehand for its burial" (Mk. 14:3–9). And then, at Gethsemane when he was so distressed and agitated, Jesus says to Peter, "Simon are you asleep? Could you not keep awake one hour?" (Mk. 14:37).

Jesus' Relationship to Other People

To his family.

It is well documented that Jesus' perception of himself in relation to his family was unusual. Luke makes this clear in his narrative of Jesus as a boy sitting amongst the teachers in the Temple and expecting his parents to understand that they would find him in his Father's house! This self-realisation of his divine kinship to God later distanced him from his house and family and caused him to ask, "Who are my mother and my brothers? Whoever does the will of God is my brother and sister and mother" (Mk. 3:31–32).

Similarly, at the wedding feast at Cana when Mary drew her son's attention to the shortage of wine, his self-awareness seemed to detach him from his mother's maternal authority. "Woman," he said, "what concern is that to you and to me? My hour is not yet come" (Jn. 2:1–4). Yet, Jesus loved his mother and ensured that she was cared for by John following the crucifixion (Jn. 19:25–27).

To his disciples

Jesus' relationship with his disciples was more complex. The Gospels make clear that he cared for them, sought to teach them many things, and defended them strongly against criticism. His questions also make clear that he expected much of them, though perhaps not always reasonably. Thus, when the disciples were at sea, afraid of perishing in the storm and they wakened Jesus, he questioned them, "Why are you afraid? Have you no faith?" (Mk. 4:35–41).

Similarly, in the storm on the Sea of Galilee when Jesus called Peter to walk towards him on the water and Peter, becoming frightened, began to sink so called out, "Lord, save me!" Jesus said to him, "You of little faith, why did you doubt?" (Mt. 14:22–23.) It seems Jesus did not always appreciate and certainly seemed not to share the ordinary human fears of his close companions.

On other occasions, he could be impatient with their simplicity, even irritated by it. Following the Parable of the Sower, for example, when the disciples and others asked Jesus about it, he said, "Do you not understand this parable? Then how will you understand all parables?" Obviously, Jesus thought the parable was easy and they should have understood (Mk. 4:13–20).

Or, when he tried to teach that it was not the unclean food that defiles a person but an unclean heart, and his disciples were puzzled, Jesus was sharp with them. "Then do you also fail to understand?" he asked. "Do you not see that whatever goes into a person from outside cannot defile, since it enters not the heart but the stomach, and goes out into the sewer?" But his disciples were simple fishermen who had been raised in a firm Jewish tradition. They had yet to gain the insight of their divine teacher (Mk. 7:17–23).

Similarly, following the miracle of feeding four thousand when the disciples were concerned because they had only one loaf with them in the boat, Jesus was irritated with them. "Why are you talking about having no bread?" he asked. "Do you still not perceive or understand? Are your hearts hardened? Do you have eyes, and fail to see? Do you have ears, and fail to hear? And do you not remember?" Then, after reminding them of the miracle, "Do you not yet understand?" (Mk. 8:14–21).

And again, when Phillip and the other disciples had simply not realised the relationship of divine union between the Father and the Son, despairingly Jesus asks, "Have I been with you all this time, Phillip, and you still do not know me? Whoever has seen me has seen the Father. How can you say, 'Show us the Father'? Do you not believe that I am in the Father and the Father is in me?" (Jn. 14:8–10). And even when the disciples did claim to believe that Jesus came from God, Jesus questioned their understanding of what he had told them. "Do you now believe?" he said, plainly doubting their grasp of what he had tried to teach them (Jn. 16:28–31).

To other people

More widely, how Jesus' saw himself in relation to many other people is again well documented in the Gospels. His empathy and compassion were widespread towards all who were in trouble or in need. However, he could be quite terse and disparaging to individuals to whom he attributed ingratitude or unfeeling righteousness.

At the healing of ten lepers, for example, he questioned, "Were not ten made clean? But the other nine, where are they? Was none of them found to return and give praise to God except this foreigner?" (Lk. 17:11–19). And in the house of Simon the Pharisee, where Jesus plainly felt he had been shabbily treated, he was scathing of his host's silent criticism towards a woman of the city who wept at Jesus' feet and had brought an alabaster jar of ointment to anoint him.

Jesus said to Simon, "Do you see this woman?" Plainly, Simon did not, and one can almost hear the scorn in Jesus' voice as he challenged Simon's total lack of perception and understanding (Lk. 7:36–50).

Towards the community collectively, 'the present generation', Jesus tended to be critical. He saw his contemporaries generally as spiritually dull, or as poor tenants of Israel, unable or unwilling to read the signs of the times. When it became clear to him that the relationship of the people to him and to the Baptist was quite negative Jesus asks, "To what then will I compare the people of this generation, and what are they like?" and he compares them to children playing in the marketplace! (Lk. 7:31–35).

Later, when it seemed obvious to Jesus that the people were simply neglecting the many signs of spiritual crisis he said, "You hypocrites! You know how to interpret the appearance of the earth and sky, but why do you not know how to interpret the present time? And why do you not judge for yourselves what is right?" (Lk. 12:56–57). And at the healing of an epileptic boy when the disciples had been unable to help, in frustration Jesus questions, "You faithless generation, how much longer must I be with you? How much longer must I put up with you?" (Mk. 9:14–29).

Undoubtedly, Jesus also saw himself as the opponent of much Jewish authority. This is clearly evident in questions he sometimes put to priests and elders in the Temple, church leaders in the Synagogues, to the Sadducees, and especially to the scribes and Pharisees. It surfaced in defence of his disciples, in the Sabbath battle, in the 'seven woes', and in the vigorous language, he sometimes used to attack his enemies.

To his environment

Jesus' human experience of 'the earth' was limited to just a small section of the planet long before science had uncovered its position in the universe or the global issues surrounding it. He travelled little about the known world but, historically, knew of Egypt, Greece, Rome, Assyria, and Babylon. He probably understood or spoke some Latin and Greek in addition to Aramaic and Hebrew. The Gospels, otherwise, are silent about his interest in art, or music, or the different religions of the world, or literature apart from apocalyptic literature and the Hebrew Bible.

What we do have from the Gospels includes the belief, common at the time, that possession by evil spirits could be the cause of illness. Exorcism might cure it, and, in this regard, Jesus understood himself to be the opponent of Satan. Otherwise, although it is not apparent in his questions, many of Jesus' parables and teachings reveal a clear awareness of Nature as it surrounded him; the lilies of the field, the sower of seeds, the tares, the mustard seed, the vine, fig trees, good fruit and bad, sheep and goats, birds of the air, the Gadarene swine, the work of fishermen, not to mention the folly of building houses on sand or putting new wine into old skins!

Also, Jesus was familiar with the wilderness, took notice of the weather signs, and often withdrew to places of quiet and tranquillity for prayers or to refresh himself.

To God

The Gospels clearly proclaim the Christian belief that Jesus is the Son of God. In some narratives, this is presented as historical commentary. In some, it emerges from the discourse between Jesus and others. In some, it stems from a realisation borne upon those who encountered Jesus.

From Luke's Gospel, we know that even as a young boy Jesus was self-conscious of a special relationship to God. In later years, his self-awareness of this unique relationship became clearer in the distinction he always maintained between 'My Father' and 'Your Father'. It was a distinction, (a 'call') which, as some of his questions revealed, resulted in distancing himself from his home and family, or caused him to chide Phillip when he failed to perceive the divine unity that linked Jesus to God, his Father.

However, Jesus never presumed upon this unity as we can see on the occasion when a man ran towards him and knelt to ask, "Good Teacher, what must I do to inherit eternal life?" Jesus replied, "Why do you call me good? No one is good but God alone."

Perhaps nothing reveals the importance to Jesus of his filial relationship to God more than his cry of spiritual anguish when, at the crucifixion, he sensed a loss of divine communion with his Father, "My God, my God, why have you forsaken me?" (Mk. 15:34).

247

End Piece

When first I began this book, it seemed a straightforward exercise and I thought I knew how it would develop. I was wrong. I was reasonably sure of my purpose but the more I studied the questions ascribed to Jesus by the Gospel writers the more I encountered unexpected and exciting discoveries. So many questions revealed unforeseen nuances.

Pictures emerged of Rabbinical discourse, of meetings in the synagogues, of life in the Temple precincts. Jesus' relationship to his disciples, to his family, to his generation was etched by his questions. Simple questions belied deep anxieties about the future of his ministry. Attacking questions disclosed undisguised anger at the hypocrisy of his opponents.

Compassionate questions are identified with the ordinary frailties of human nature. And the Gospels themselves threw light onto the development of the church. Jesus' questions in Mark, so reflective of his human nature; in Matthew, of the Church's understanding of Jesus; in John, of the Church's reflection on the event of Jesus.

From all of this emerged the totally unexpected perception of Jesus as a person. That was an undeserved gift so characteristic of the grace of our Lord in his long engagement with those who worship him. I hope readers enjoy the book and find it helpful.

Select Bibliography

Allen, W. C. (1985) *St Matthew*. International Critical Commentary, Edinburgh: T. & T. Clark.

Balmforth, H. (1933) *Saint Luke*. The Clarendon Bible (Wild & Box (eds.)), Oxford: Clarendon.

Bernard, J. H. (1985) *St John*. International Critical Commentary, Edinburgh: T. & T. Clark.

Blunt, A. F. W. (1949) *Saint Mark*. The Clarendon Bible (Strong & Wild (eds.)), Oxford: Clarendon.

Bruce, F. T. (1983) *The Hard Sayings of Jesus*. (The Jesus Library (M. Green (ed.))), London: Hodder & Stoughton.

Buchanan, D. (1988) *The Counselling of Jesus*. (The Jesus Library (M. Green (ed.))), London: Hodder & Stoughton.

Cole, R. A. (1983) *Mark*. Tyndale New Testament Commentaries, Leicester: Inter-varsity Press.

Copenhaver, M. (2014) *Jesus Is the Question*, Nashville: Abingdon Press.

Cross, F. L. & Livingstone, E. A., 1983, *The Oxford Dictionary of the Christian Church,* Oxford University Press.

Dear, J. (2004) *The Questions of Jesus*, Melbourne: Image Publishing Group.

Dias, E. (2015) *What Did Jesus Ask?* Time Home Publisher Entertainment.

Evans, C. F. (1990) *Saint Luke.* TPI New Testament Commentaries (H. C. Kee and D. Nineham (eds.)), London: SCM Press.

Funk, N. & Menze, M. (2014) *Questions Jesus Asked.* Create Space Independent Publishing Platform.

Gould, E. P. (1983) *St Mark.* International Critical Commentary, Edinburgh: T. & T. Clark.

Green, F. W. (1947) *Saint Matthew.* The Clarendon Bible (Strong & Wild (eds.)), Oxford: Clarendon.

Harper, M. (1985) *The Healings of Jesus.* (The Jesus Library. (M. Green (ed.))), London: Hodder & Stoughton.

Harris, D. (2003) *Devotional Meditations on the Questions of Jesus,* Maitland: Xulon Press.

Harvey, N. P. (1991) *The Morals of Jesus,* London: Darton, Longman & Todd.

Hastings, J. (1914) *Dictionary of the Bible,* Edinburgh: T. & T. Clark.

Jeremias, J. (1976) *The Prayers of Jesus,* SCM Press.

Larsen, D. & Larsen, S. (2019) *Questions Jesus Asks.* (Lifeguide Bible Studies), IVP Connect.

Marshall, J. A. (2002) *But Who Do You Say That I Am?* (Ambassador Books), Worcester, Massachusetts.

Monday Morning Review (2020) *135 Questions Jesus Asked.* (online) Available at: <https://mondaymorningreview.wordpress.com/2010/05/14/137questionsjesusasked/> (Accessed 17 June 2020).

Plummer, A. (1909) *St Luke.* International Critical Commentary, Edinburgh: T. & T. Clark.

Pope C. (2020) *100 Questions Jesus Asked and You Ought to Answer - Community In Mission.* (online) Community in Mission. Available at: <http://blog.adw.org/2012/02/100-questions-jesus-asked-and-you-ought-to-answer/> (Accessed 17 June 2020).

Rackham, R. B. (1912) *The Acts of the Apostle.* Westminster Commentaries (W. Lock (ed.)), Methuen.

Rawlinson, A. E. J. (1925) *The Gospel According to St Mark.* Westminster Commentaries (W. Lock (ed.)), Methuen.

Taylor, V. (1957) *The Gospel According to St Mark*, London: MacMillan.

The New Oxford Annotated Bible (New Revised Standard Version) (1991) Oxford University Press.

Throckmorton, B. H. ((ed.)) (1992) *Gospel Parallels,* London: Thomas Nelson. Tiede, B., *339 Questions Jesus Asked.* https;//leadingwithquestions.com/tag/339-questions-jesus-asked. (Accessed 17 July 2020).

Westcott, B. F. (1881) *The Gospel According to St John*, London: Murray.